VICTORY IN WESTERN EUROPE

VICTORY IN WESTERN EUROPE

From D-Day to the Nazi Surrender

G.E. PATRICK MURRAY

Series Editor: Lieutenant Colonel Roger Cirillo, United States Army, Retired

MetroBooks

MetroBooks

An Imprint of Friedman/Fairfax Publishers

©1999 by Michael Friedman Publishing
Group, Inc.

Library of Congress Cataloging-in-Publication
Data available upon request.
ISBN 1-56799-759-7

Editor: Celeste Sollod
Art Director: Kevin Ullrich
Photography Editor: Amy Talluto
Production Manager: Camille Lee

Color separations by Ocean Graphic Arts Ltd.
Printed in China by Leefung Asco Printers Ltd.

10 9 8 7 6 5 4 3 2 1

For bulk purchases and special sales,
please contact:
Friedman/Fairfax Publishers
Attention: Sales Department
15 West 26th Street
New York, NY 10010
212/685-6610 FAX 212/685-1307

Visit our website:
http://www.metrobooks.com

Dedication

To Jacqué, who makes it all worthwhile

Acknowledgments

My thanks go to my good friend who suggested yet another book for me to write: Lt. Col. Roger Cirillo, USA (Ret.); to Col. Victor Infortuna, FMC; and to my editors at Michael Friedman Publishing Group, Ms. Sharyn Rosart and Ms. Celeste Sollod.

Contents

Foreword **The Great Crusade** 8

Introduction **The War Prior to D-Day** 10

Chapter 1 **The Invasion of Normandy** 12

Chapter 2 **German Defeat in France** 36

Chapter 3 **The Race to the West Wall** 60

Chapter 4 **The Battle of the Bulge** 80

Chapter 5 **The Defeat of Germany** 100

Bibliography 124

Index 125

The Great Crusade

Lt. Col. Roger Cirillo, USA (Ret.)

Far from shore, loudspeakers on more than 5,000 ships in mid-Channel blared the Supreme Allied Commander's words: "Soldiers, sailors, and airmen of the Allied Expeditionary Force! You are about to embark upon The Great Crusade...." Similar scenes were enacted on airfields, in embarkation areas, and at headquarters scattered throughout England, all supporting the great invasion armada bearing down on France. It was June 6, 1944—D-Day.

Since Caesar's time, great armies have been sent into battle with their commander's words echoing in their ears—some flowery, some profane, many designed for the benefit of posterity rather than for the warriors about to enter combat. The words of General Dwight D. Eisenhower, however, were different from those of other commanders, just as The Great Crusade differed from many other battles. Eisenhower, the military champion of this Crusade, was the human symbol of a great allied force that had swept two continents to end the greatest tyranny of modern times. Ike's words were genuine, and the men and women who marched, flew, or sailed as part of his four-million-strong force believed in him and in the cause.

The insignia used for his Supreme Allied Headquarters represented the idealism of the force he commanded. It pictured a flaming Crusader's sword, a sword of liberation, placed on a black field representing the darkness of Nazi oppression. Above it, a rainbow of colors taken from the Allies' national flags spread out under a wider swath of blue, symbolizing the peace and tranquillity that the Allies sought to return to Europe.

The Great Crusade followed a long road to Normandy. While the Americans considered the cross-channel attack the centerpiece of Allied strategy and had agreed to a "Germany first" strategy (in which they would fight Japan after Germany), the American people, enraged by the Japanese attack on Pearl Harbor, demanded a strong Pacific response. Shipping was not yet available to support both offensives in decisive numbers, and American industry had yet to reach its peak capacity, so the European theater had to wait.

The Great Crusade also had to await two other key campaigns—the Battle of the Atlantic and the air war. In 1942 and 1943, German submarines imperiled Great Britain's survival and were a great danger to the movement of troops and matériel. Prior to late spring 1943, when the Atlantic battle for superiority at sea turned in favor of the Allies, the ability to stage, mount, and supply the forces that were needed to attack the continent directly would have been severely threatened by U-boats. Also in 1943, the mighty daylight air armada needed to destroy the Luftwaffe (the Nazi air force) and to attack Germany's means of production had not yet moved overseas. While Britain's Royal Air Force conducted nightly raids into Germany, the American bomber force was still small in numbers. Adolf Hitler had referred to Europe as Festung Europa ("Fortress Europe"), but by the spring of 1944, Allied airmen fulfilled their task of achieving air superiority over Europe. In their words, they had "put a roof over it."

Least palatable to the Americans in 1943, but certainly true, was the fact that America's great citizen army was not yet ready to fight the veteran Wehrmacht (the German army). America's equipment and tactics, and importantly, the selection and seasoning of its commanders, still needed fine-tuning. The Americans lacked the experience that only combat could bring. The evolutionary change required for them to go against the Germans was accomplished in North Africa and the Mediterranean against enemy forces limited by geography and supply, a plus that would not be granted in open battle in France. Eisenhower and his commanders developed their war fighting skills in the 1943 Mediterranean campaign. Likewise, American tactics and equipment were improved, changes that were to prove decisive in the fields of Europe.

The Great Crusade benefited greatly from its Russian allies. The Soviet Union bore the brunt of Hitler's strength; Germany pitted 165 of her divisions against a mobilized Russian force of about 19 million men and women, 6 million of whom manned the battle line. Germany had attacked the Russian bear in its lair and was unable to back away. The strategic drain meant that fully three–quarters of Germany's forces, supplies, and industry were aimed at maintaining the eastern front—a force imbalance that made The Great Crusade possible in June 1944.

Russia's contribution was costly. The eastern front was said to have claimed an average of 15,000 Russian lives per day in the fiercest fighting seen anywhere during World War II. The Russians had been awaiting a major second front for two and a half years. While the western Allies viewed D-Day, the liberation of Paris, the Battle of the Bulge, and the Rhine crossing as bringing an end to Hitler's tyranny, the greatest down payment on victory was made in eastern Europe, and the Russian people must be remembered as the Allies who suffered most.

The Great Crusade illustrated America's rising tide of power, but it by no means meant that the smaller British Commonwealth, Free French, Dutch, or Polish contingents contributed any less. Each performed on a scale proportional to its country's size and capability, and those under the bombs and shells, whether in Britain, France, the Netherlands, or Luxembourg, all suffered greatly and spent years rebuilding their homelands. The Great Crusade was an Allied victory and a triumph of free men everywhere fighting to stay free.

ABOVE: A British Buffalo amphibious vehicle exits its Landing Craft Tank (LCT) on November 1, 1944, during operations against Germans on Walcheren Island at the mouth of the Scheldt Estuary, in Holland. The two-month delay in opening Antwerp to ship traffic remains one of the most controversial issues of the campaign in northwest Europe. RIGHT: French-Canadian soldiers of the Regiment de Maisonneuve advance toward Rijssen on April 9, 1945. By that time, the residents of German-occupied Holland were experiencing famine conditions due to the occupation.

The War Prior to D-Day

On September 1, 1939, German tanks crossed the border into Poland. Two days later Britain and France declared war on Germany. "Be hard," Hitler told his generals on August 22, concerning the attack on Poland, "Be without mercy. The citizens of Western Europe must quiver in terror." Employing massed tank formations with mechanized infantry and artillery plus fighter-bomber support, the Germans gave birth to what became known as the Blitzkrieg—lightning war.

In payment for its nonaggression pact with Germany of August 23, the Soviets gained half of Poland on September 17. A lull in the fighting known as the "phony war" occurred in the winter of 1939–40, lasting until April, when the Germans invaded Denmark and Norway. On May 10, 1940, the German army invaded France and the low countries, drove the British out of France at Dunkirk, and defeated the French army, which outnumbered the German force and had better tanks. Hitler's Blitzkrieg achieved in six weeks' time what Germany had been unable to achieve in four years in World War I.

From 1940 to 1941, Britain stood alone. Russia continued its nonaggression policy with Germany, while the United States was neutral but rearming. After the German air force failed to gain command of the air over the English Channel in the Battle of Britain,

Hitler canceled his planned invasion of England and in June 1941 invaded the Soviet Union. Six months later and half a world away, Germany's ally Japan bombed both Singapore and Pearl Harbor in one day. Days later Hitler and Benito Mussolini declared war on America. The conflict was now truly a world war.

Immediately after Pearl Harbor, Prime Minister Winston Churchill and the British Chiefs of Staff (COS) flew to Washington, D.C., for talks with President Franklin D. Roosevelt and the American military. By prior agreement Anglo-American policy was to fight Germany first and to remain on the defensive against Japan. To coordinate the war in the Atlantic and the Mediterranean and to implement policy, the Anglo-Americans established the Combined Chiefs of Staff (CCS), which had its office in Washington, D.C., throughout the war.

The United States was compelled to organize its own military committee, the Joint Chiefs of Staff (JCS), to meet with the British Chiefs. The establishment of the JCS and the CCS was a giant step that helped make the Anglo-American alliance the most successful military partnership ever. Differences in national outlook occurred, but the cooperation of Britain and America had to do with their common history, language, and tradition. The only thing these countries had in common with the Soviet Union was their enemy, Adolf Hitler.

The "Second Front"

In 1941 Soviet leader Joseph Stalin was the senior statesman of the so-called Big Three (Stalin, Roosevelt, and Churchill), and the Red Army was the world's largest army. Inefficient and ineffective since Stalin had purged its officer corps in the late thirties, the Red Army lost three million men, killed or taken prisoner between June and December. Incredibly, the Russians counterattacked in December and drove the Germans back from Moscow. Russia was spared defeat in 1941, but it still faced virtually three fourths of the German army in 1942 and only slightly less in 1943. Stalin issued his first calls for an Anglo-American "second front" in 1942 to draw off some German troops from the eastern front.

A second front meant a cross-channel invasion to both Stalin and the American military planners. U.S. planners wanted an

ABOVE: President Franklin D. Roosevelt and Prime Minister Winston Churchill met in Casablanca, Morocco, on January 31, 1943, to plan strategy against the Axis powers. OPPOSITE: Top Nazi leaders assemble in Berlin in May 1938, prior to their departure for talks with the Italian dictator Benito Mussolini in Italy. Hermann Göring, commander of the German air force, stands to Hitler's right, while Propaganda Minister Joseph Goebbels is on Hitler's left; Heinrich Himmler, commander of the SS, is on Goebbels' left.

invasion of France followed by a drive on the Ruhr, the industrial heart of Germany, which was about 250 miles (400km) from the Pas de Calais (the area around Calais itself). President Roosevelt feared that unless American troops were fighting Germans by the end of 1942, the American people's hatred of the Japanese caused by Pearl Harbor might weaken the Germany-first decision.

Roosevelt promised the Russians a second front in 1942, but Britain preferred a peripheral strategy, what Churchill called "closing the ring"—the bombing, sabotage, and raiding of Europe's German-occupied coastline—to a direct invasion. Kicked out of Norway, France, Greece, and Crete, the British were understandably reluctant to take on the Germans in northwest Europe until the British and Americans were far stronger, and the Germans were far weaker. The British had no intention of launching a cross-channel invasion in 1942, as such an attack was beyond their capability. Therefore, while the British dominated strategic decisions from 1942 through 1943, the Anglo-American war effort rousted out Germans from North Africa, Sicily, and southern Italy. Opening the Mediterranean and the Suez Canal to the Indian Ocean eliminated the need to sail around the Cape of Good Hope (South Africa), cut in half Britain's journey to India, and cut by three quarters the journey to Egypt. This vastly increased the efficiency of Britain's merchant marine. Further-more, by May 1943 the Anglo-Americans had gained the upper hand in the Atlantic Ocean in the struggle with German submarines. The Allies were finally poised to return to Europe to take on the German Wehrmacht. This is the story of the last year of World War II in northwest Europe, from June 1944 to May 1945.

Chapter 1

The Invasion of Normandy

AT 5:20 A.M. ON TUESDAY, JUNE 6, 1944, THE SUN ROSE OVER THE BAY OF THE
Seine, on the north coast of France. German soldiers manning a 60-mile (96km) stretch of Hitler's
Atlantic Wall from the Cotentin Peninsula to Ouistreham saw the armada of the democracies
stretching from one end of the horizon to the other. More than 5,000 ships and craft were set to
land 175,000 men and 50,000 vehicles. Within fifteen minutes an Allied air armada of 11,000
planes would begin bombing and strafing German positions on the beaches and coastal towns of
Normandy. Operation Overlord, the long-awaited hope of millions in occupied Europe, had begun.

Overlord, the code name for the invasion of Normandy, was a giant first step in the campaign
that liberated western Europe from Nazi tyranny. Winston Churchill, prime minister of Britain,
said that the German rule in Europe marked "the abyss of the new dark age." Overlord marked
the end of the abyss. The Allied landings signaled Hitler's
Götterdämmerung, the twilight of Hitler's gods—racism, power,
and death—and in Hitler's twilight millions more died.

The Supreme Commander of the Allied Expeditionary Force

The Anglo-American military defeat of Germany was extraordi-
narily difficult. Fortunately the Anglo-American military coalition
was also the most successful such alliance in history, largely
because of the talents of the American general who led it.

LEFT: Troops wade ashore
toward the terror of Omaha
Beach around 7:30 a.m. on
D-Day, June 6, 1944; the
plateau above the beach is
already on fire. The men of
the 1st Infantry Division are
approaching a tank that has
landed just ahead of them.

The Supreme Commander: General Dwight D. Eisenhower

Dwight David Eisenhower, one of six sons of David and Ida Eisenhower, grew up in Abilene, Kansas. Like his classmate Omar Bradley, Eisenhower went to West Point because it was free. He graduated in the Class of 1915, known as the "Class the Stars Fell On," because nearly 60 of its 164 graduates became general officers.

A colonel in September 1941, Eisenhower became a four-star general seventeen months later, in February 1943. He would be named General of the Army (five stars) on December 16, 1944, the day the Germans began the Battle of the Bulge. Warm, outgoing, and famous for his smile, Eisenhower controlled his temper and got along with his British counterparts. In fact, Eisenhower came to personify the Anglo-American alliance.

The night before D-Day, General Eisenhower wrote a note he never had to use: "My decision to attack at this time and place was based upon the best information available. The troops, the air and the Navy did all that bravery and devotion to duty could do. If any blame or fault attaches to the attempt, it is mine alone."

German Minister of Armaments Albert Speer inspects the Atlantic Wall, designed to protect Fortress Europe, which cost nearly four billion German marks and consumed seventeen million cubic yards (13 million cubic meters) of concrete. In his memoirs, Speer called the cost and effort "sheer waste."

Both President Franklin D. Roosevelt and Prime Minister Churchill had promised the command of Overlord to the chiefs of their respective armies, Gen. George C. Marshall and Field Marshal Sir Alan Brooke. However, by 1943 Roosevelt and Churchill had agreed that an American general should command Overlord because Americans would eventually outnumber the British in the expeditionary force four to one. Roosevelt thought he could not part with Marshall's strategic gifts and political influence with Congress, so he started

searching for the most likely American commander for the Allied forces.

Maj. Gen. Dwight D. Eisenhower would have seemed an unlikely choice to command an Allied invasion when he arrived in London in June 1942 to take over the European Theater of Operations' U.S. Army. Eisenhower had been a staff officer most of his career; he had never heard a shot fired in battle and had little command experience. He was in England to talk the British into supporting a cross-channel invasion in 1942,

in which the American contribution would be a paltry two divisions out of a total fifteen. The British had committed themselves to a buildup in the British Isles in 1942 in preparation for a cross-channel invasion in 1943, and that was where matters stood when Eisenhower arrived in London. However, the fall of Tobruk, Libya, to the Germans on June 20, 1942, changed everything.

Churchill was visiting the White House when the garrison at Tobruk, on the north coast of Libya, surrendered after a lengthy siege. Roosevelt sent Harry Hopkins, his top aide; Gen. Marshall; and Adm. Ernest J. King, chief of naval operations, to London to firm up plans for a cross-channel invasion, but the British absolutely refused that course of action and after three days of haggling, the Americans consented to an invasion of North Africa in the fall. Roosevelt had to get American troops fighting Germans somewhere by the November elections or risk repudiation of the Democrats at the polls and the future of his government's Germany-first decision. North Africa in 1942 was hardly a second front, but it would have to do.

Because the British had destroyed the French fleet to prevent the Germans from seizing it, they thought it would be a good idea for an American general to command the invasion of French North Africa. Hopefully, the French would take more kindly to an American-led invasion of their colonies than one led by the seemingly "perfidious Albion." Looking around for someone to command Operation Torch, as it was code-named, King suggested Eisenhower. Ironically, Eisenhower would thus command an invasion he opposed on the grounds that it would prevent the 1943 cross-channel invasion.

The landings in North Africa did lead to the cancellation of a 1943 cross-channel invasion, and Eisenhower went on to head two more Mediterranean invasions, in Sicily and southern Italy, which toppled Mussolini but drew off trifling numbers of Germans from the eastern front. At the first meeting of Churchill, Roosevelt, and Stalin, at the Teheran Conference in November 1943, Stalin bluntly demanded to know the name of the officer who was to command the invasion of Europe. A week later, in December 1943, Roosevelt told Eisenhower, "Well, Ike—you'd better start packing."

General Sir Bernard Law Montgomery

Bernard Montgomery was the fourth of nine children born to Rev. Henry and Maud Montgomery. He attended St. Paul's School in London and as commanding general made his 21st Army Group Headquarters there prior to the Normandy invasion.

A graduate of the Royal Military Academy, Sandhurst, he was severely wounded and won the DSO (Distinguished Service Order) in World War I. He commanded a corps at Dunkirk in 1940. As commander of the British Eighth Army that defeated Rommel's Afrika Korps at the battle of El Alamein in November 1942, Montgomery became the most famous British general of the war. He was well known by his trademark black tanker's beret, sweaters, and corduroy pants and for being tactless. Churchill had him promoted to field marshal on September 1, 1944.

Made a viscount in 1946, he chose the title Viscount Montgomery of Alamein.

Britain's most famous soldier of World War II, Bernard Law Montgomery, still inspires adulation in Britain. However, headstrong and forthright, he was a difficult man to serve over, as Eisenhower found out.

The first meeting of the Big Three (Stalin, Roosevelt, and Churchill) occurred in November 1943, at Teheran, Iran, because Stalin refused to go anywhere else. Marshal Stalin, on the left, is greeting Prime Minister Churchill's daughter, Sarah. President Roosevelt is seated in the center, with Churchill to his left.

Eisenhower packed. After a trip home to confer with Roosevelt and Marshall, and to see his wife, Mamie Doud Eisenhower, he returned to London in mid-January 1944 to set up his headquarters, known as SHAEF (Supreme Headquarters Allied Expeditionary Force). All of the commanders of Eisenhower's forces were British and had extensive command and combat experience. Adm. Sir Bertram Ramsay commanded the naval forces, and Air Chief Marshal Sir Trafford Leigh-Mallory led the air forces. Gen. Bernard Law Montgomery, commanding general of the British 21st Army Group, would command the ground forces until Eisenhower moved his headquarters to the continent. Eisenhower's deputy supreme commander was Air Chief Marshal of the Royal Air Force Sir Arthur Tedder; his chief of staff was an American, Lt. Gen. Walter Bedell Smith.

The Plan

The predecessor to SHAEF was COSSAC, Chief of Staff Supreme Allied Command, the commander designate of which was Lt. Gen. Sir Frederick Morgan.

COSSAC's 1943 plan was essentially a feasibility study that evolved into Overlord. Morgan selected Normandy because it was within range of RAF Spitfires based in England and its fortifications were far less formidable than those of the Pas de Calais. As a result of the August 1942 German defeat of the Canadian raid on the heavily defended Channel port of Dieppe, Morgan planned to land on beaches. Normandy had a port, Cherbourg, at the top of the Cotentin Peninsula, but the Allies also intended to bring pre-fabricated ports known as Mulberries, a giant British project that cost around $100 million, that would enable the Allies to land on the beaches where they did not already hold parts.

Geography and ports determined where the two national armies would land in France under COSSAC's plan. Since the U.S. Army's embarkation points were in southwestern England and the army would receive both supplies and new divisions through Cherbourg and the Brittany ports, and later directly from the United States, American forces landed on the western, or right, flank of Normandy at the so code-named Utah and Omaha Beaches. British and Canadian forces, which embarked from southeastern England, landed on the eastern, or left, flank at the so code-named Gold, Juno, and Sword Beaches. The British and Canadians would capture Channel ports for their resupply.

On June 6, 1944, D-Day, the Normandy campaign began with the largest amphibious landing in military history.

Hitler wanted to bottle up the Allies in Normandy for as long as possible because doing so presented the shortest possible line of defense for German forces engaged in fighting in Russia, Italy, and now France. Once the Allies broke out of Normandy, the Germans would be hard pressed to hold onto a broad front.

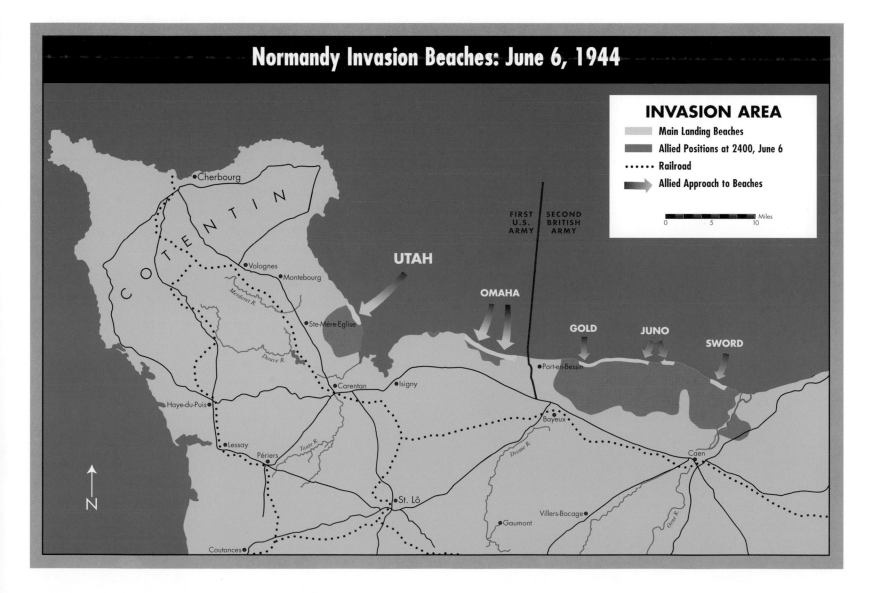

The Shortage of Landing Craft

The Supreme Allied Commander's greatest problem was the shortage of landing craft. Churchill summed it up: "The destinies of two great empires . . . seem to be tied up in some goddamned things called LSTs." Landing Ship Tanks (LSTs) were a British solution to landing tanks or trucks on a beach. Infantry needed tanks to take out machine guns, overcome barbwire, and provide moral support. The question was how to get them onto the beach.

In early 1941 the British provided the Americans with designs for a ship over 300 feet (92m) in length that could lift 2,000 tons (1,800t), which meant it could easily unload more than two dozen Sherman tanks, but the U.S. Navy had no interest until after Pearl Harbor. However, by the end of the war, the Anglo-American forces had built more than 46,000 landing vessels of all types, with the United States building ten times the British total, yet there were never enough landing craft, owing to their low construction priority in comparison to aircraft carriers, destroyers, cruisers, and submarines.

LSTs were the naval equivalent of a moving van and a car carrier. The CCS had told Gen. Morgan that he would have only enough craft to sea lift (transport across the Channel) a three-division assault, but Gen. Montgomery refused to command less than a five-division force. Eisenhower also wanted a five-division landing, so he postponed the landings from May to June to gain an extra month's production of landing craft; he also postponed the simultaneous invasion of southern France, code-named Anvil (later called Operation Dragoon). Postponements allowed enough time to produce sea lift and repair enough craft for a five-division assault.

An American Landing Ship Tank (LST) demonstrates the delivery of an M-4 Sherman tank during maneuvers in 1944 off the east coast of the United States. By dropping stern anchors, LSTs could winch themselves off beaches, but in Normandy they simply allowed the tides to lift them off.

Ultra and the Deception Plans

The postponement of the invasion, due to a shortage of landing craft, gave SHAEF deception teams another month to convince the Germans that the primary landing would occur in the Pas de Calais, so that the Germans would keep the Fifteenth Army's panzer reserves above the Seine.

The deception plan benefited from the British ability to listen to what one German headquarters said to another. Before the war, the Poles had given the British a German Enigma cipher machine, which ultimately allowed the British to read German orders and plans for much of the war. Ultra, short for Ultra Secret, was the name for intercepted German radio signals. Throughout the eleven-month campaign in Europe, Ultra provided the German order of battle (number and type of formations), plans, and movements. Combining Ultra with the work of the Twenty Committee (XX), known as "Double Cross," the Allies could judge the success of their deception. (The British had arrested German agents in the United Kingdom and forced them to work for Britain, hence the name "Double Cross.") The Twenty Committee fed a steady diet of misleading intelligence to the Abwehr, the German intelligence service. Following one of these fictitious reports on June 10, the First SS Panzer Division actually turned around and returned to its base in the Pas de Calais.

Strategic bombers also helped deceive the Germans, while the bombing served to isolate Normandy and the Pas de Calais from the rest of France. Under the Transportation Plan, American B-17s and B-24s and RAF Lancasters dropped thousands of tons of bombs on the French rail system's marshaling yards, tracks, and road cuts; medium bombers and fighter-bombers went after locomotives, rolling stock, bridges, and tunnels. As part of the deception, the Allied air forces dropped two tons of bombs north of the Seine for every ton dropped south of the Seine.

Churchill was appalled by a study that predicted the campaign might kill 40,000 French citizens. When the Anglo-Americans consulted Lt. Gen. Marie Pierre Koenig, head of the French Forces of the Interior, about this possibility of mass deaths of his citizens, he replied,

"This is war," and the invasion went on. Most studies cite 10,000 French deaths resulting from the bombing and the invasion. Given the population density of France, and the level of effort involved (12,000 Allied airmen were killed and 2,000 planes lost), that figure seems far too low to be realistic.

The Germans

The weather in June 1944 was the worst in forty years, and the weather forecast for June 5 was so ominous that Eisenhower postponed the invasion, adding to the Allies' tactical surprise. Assuming an invasion required five consecutive days of good weather, German Field

LEFT, TOP: First produced in the 1920s to protect business secrets, the Enigma machine was adopted by the Wehrmacht as its signals cryptographic machine. The British ability to decode the machine's ciphers was the "ultra" secret; it was first made public in 1974.
LEFT, BOTTOM: A panoramic view of the coast of France in July 1944 at low tide shows the depth of defenses that Allied infantry had to cross under German fire. Defenses in Normandy were about 20 percent complete by June 1944, while those in the Pas de Calais were nearly 80 percent complete.

American gliders, such as these Wacos, ferried in equipment for the 82nd Airborne Division behind Utah Beach. Gliders were essentially disposable craft; 3,300 were used in the invasion.

Marshal Erwin Rommel drove home to see his wife on her birthday, June 6. German planes and patrol boats stood down, and senior German commanders went to Rennes, in Brittany, on June 5 to take part in a war game; paratroopers of the American 101st Airborne killed one of these generals coming back in the dark.

Morale was poor in the German high command. Field Marshal Gerd von Rundstedt, Commander in Chief West, the oldest officer in the army, looked down on Hitler, whom he called that "corporal," referring to the Führer's World War I rank. The Prussian aristocrat found his subordinate Rommel, Army Group B commander, tiring and referred to him as *Marschall Bubi*, "the boy marshal."

Rommel had ordered millions of mines laid in 1944. Thousands of beach obstacles between high and low water sprouted Teller (plate-shaped) mines to rip boats apart or blow them up. Also on his orders, millions of tons of concrete went into casements, block houses, pill-boxes, and bunkers, but it is difficult to believe that Rommel thought that the Atlantic Wall would be any more effective than the Maginot Line had been in 1940. Having fought in North Africa, Rommel was certain that Allied aerial supremacy would make it impossible for

the Germans to move their panzer reserves from the interior of France. The Germans had to defeat the invasion at the water's edge.

Von Rundstedt thought that the Atlantic Wall was a colossal waste, but his experience in Russia left him unprepared for the weight of Anglo-American air power. He considered it lunacy for Rommel to advocate fighting, using thin-skinned panzers within range of naval gunfire. Allied destroyers had blasted German tanks on the invasion beaches of Sicily and Anzio. Therefore, von Rundstedt believed that Germany's panzers had to be positioned to attack the flank of any Allied invasion as it emerged from either Normandy or the Pas de Calais. When the two officers appealed their differences to Hitler, the Führer created a panzer reserve, which he alone commanded; his staff, however, refused to wake him up on D-Day when von Rundstedt's headquarters called at 4:00 a.m. Subsequently, there was no German armored counterattack until 4:00 p.m.

On June 5, 1944, the German army had sixty divisions in France, and while Normandy had nine infantry divisions, or one fifth of the infantry, the area had only one panzer division, or one tenth of the tanks. There were two panzer divisions within half a day's march

What the U.S. Airborne Carried

Members of nearly all airborne troops carried M-1 Garand rifles and wore uniforms that included a helmet, gloves, and boots. Each soldier also carried a pocket knife, a trench knife, a hunting knife, rations, a flashlight, a spoon, a razor, a compass, maps, one cartridge belt, two bandoliers of machine-gun ammo (676 rounds of .30 caliber and 66 rounds of .45 caliber), two fragmentation grenades, a smoke grenade, an antitank mine, a 2-pound (.9kg) Gammon grenade (plastic explosive intended to kill tanks), a .45 automatic, a water canteen, a shovel, three first-aid kits and two morphine needles, a bayonet, a main parachute, a reserve parachute, a gas mask, underwear, four TNT sticks and two blasting caps, a Mae West (a life preserver, nicknamed for the full-figured actress), an orange panel for aerial recognition, a blanket, a raincoat, and two cartons of cigarettes. Most men carried over a hundred pounds (45kg).

from Normandy. Much of the infantry in Normandy were *Osttruppen*, eastern troops: captured anti-Red Russians. Because of their critical manpower needs at this stage of the war, many German garrisons featured so-called stomach battalions, that is, men with ulcers culled from the rest of the army, who were fed a bland diet while waiting to fight in place. However, one actual German infantry unit, the 352nd Division, had taken up a position behind Omaha Beach and remained undetected by Allied intelligence until hours before the invasion.

Gen. Eisenhower flashes his famous grin while talking to paratroopers of the 101st Airborne Division moments before they take off for Normandy on the evening of June 5, 1944. To Eisenhower's left is his British military assistant, Lt. Col. James Gault. Notice that wartime censors have cut out all identifying insignia and patches.

The Allied Airborne Divisions

The first Allied soldiers invaded Normandy in the dark. Shortly after midnight three of six British gliders put down in a field between the Bénouville bridge at the Caen Canal and the Ranville bridge over the Orne River, on the eastern flank of the invasion behind Sword Beach. Within twenty minutes Maj. John Howard's men of the 6th British Airborne had taken both bridges and within an hour they had stopped a German counterattack with two tanks.

On the western flank, inexperienced pilots let down the American 101st and the 82nd Airborne Divisions

An American paratrooper climbs aboard a transport plane in England prior to the nightdrop of June 5-6, 1944. His load allowed him to fight for two days without resupply. The .45 caliber Thompson submachine gun weighed eleven pounds and carried twenty bullet clips.

over a fifteen- by twenty-five-mile (24×40km) area of the lower Cotentin Peninsula behind Utah Beach. Paratroopers carried their light personal weapons, but their radios, bazookas, and mortars went into equipment bags with their parachutes; 40 percent of these were lost in the drop.

The 82nd took Ste. Mère-Eglise, the first French town to be liberated; one of its privates, John Steele, played dead as his chute caught on the church steeple. Steele was wounded, deafened by the church bell that rang throughout the battle, and later captured. Farther east, many men drowned in the grassy swamps along the Merderet River that Rommel had flooded for just such an eventuality. During the night, the 101st seized the beach exits behind Utah Beach, linking up with the American 4th Infantry Division in the morning.

ABOVE: American troops debark from a Landing Craft Tank (LCT) at Les Dunes de Madeleine on Utah Beach on D-Day. RIGHT: Troops wade ashore in Normandy on D-Day after the beach has been taken. Note that many of the soldiers are carrying stretchers.

Utah Beach

SHAEF expected that Utah Beach would have the heaviest casualties, but the westernmost right-flank landing on D-Day turned out to be the safest; fewer than 200 men were lost there.

Strong currents had pushed the landing craft 2,000 yards (1,800m) south of their target, and a group of officers had gathered to look at a map, when Brig. Gen. Theodore Roosevelt, Jr., President Theodore Roosevelt's son and the assistant division commander, walked up. Glancing at the map and the beach exits he said, "We'll start the war from right here." The 4th Division's accidental landing spot enabled the troops to outflank stronger German defenses and get beyond the beach.

Omaha Beach

Omaha Beach was nearly a disaster. The 1st Infantry Division and the 29th Infantry Division took the highest casualties of the invasion; more than 2,000 men were killed at Omaha. None of the troops had expected to run into the German 352nd Division.

Because German artillery could still hit targets on Utah Beach, as seen here on June 11, 1944, thereby threatening unloading operations, Maj. Gen. J. Lawton Collins, VII Corps commander, strengthened his attack up the Cotentin Peninsula to quickly eliminate German artillery.

Troops from a 1st Infantry Division support unit pose aboard a ship before sailing for the continent. Some of these men are obviously vehicle drivers, judging from the goggles on their helmets. The lone African-American soldier, wearing a different style jacket, is likely from a support engineer brigade.

ABOVE, LEFT: Germans put their Teller (plate) antitank mines on small tree trunks. Placed between high and low water about 250 yards (457m) from shore at the first line of defense, such mines would blow up a small landing craft and damage larger boats. The Allies avoided most of these devices by landing at low tide, when the mines were clearly visible. ABOVE, RIGHT: Casemented 88mm guns at Utah Beach were shielded from the sea by the concrete pier. They were designed to kill soldiers and craft by firing obliquely down the beach rather than out to sea. LEFT: A boat full of men approaches Omaha Beach while the battle rages; at this point the beach was becoming increasingly crowded.

Only five of the thirty-two DD (duplex drive) tanks with tracks and propellers made it to the beach. When their LCTs (Landing Craft Tanks) unloaded them 6,000 yards (5,500m) out in five-foot (1.5m) seas, twenty-seven DD tanks filled with water above their waterproof curtains and promptly sank. Nearly all the dukws (amphibious trucks) carrying artillery pieces sank. Thus, the artillery support that the infantry was told to expect, and which was received on all the other beaches, did not make it to Omaha.

Improvisation by the U.S. Navy saved the day. Junior officers began beaching their LCTs to get tanks and vehicles ashore, but by 8:30 a.m. the Navy beach masters halted all landings at the couple of beach channels that had been cleared of obstacles. At 9:50 a.m. the answer to the half-drowned, confused survivors behind the seawall came in the shape of a five-inch (13cm) gun.

LEFT: Late on D-Day, troops land safely behind half-tracks and an amphibious truck, known as a dukw. Dukw was a name developed by General Motors engineers that is supposed to stand for the following: D for 1942; U for utility; K for front-wheel drive; W for two rear driving axles. Actually, the initials are completely arbitrary; the engineers simply wanted a name for the vehicle that sounded like duck, as the truck swam in water and walked on land, like that animal. OPPOSITE LEFT: U.S. Rangers at Pointe du Hoc scaled the cliff with rope ladders to reach German heavy guns. OPPOSITE RIGHT: Brig. Gen. Theodore Roosevelt, Jr., assistant division commander of the 4th Infantry Division, died of a heart attack on July 12, 1944, just as Gen. Eisenhower was about to promote him. Roosevelt walked with a cane and was one of the oldest combat officers in the army.

Adm. C.F. Bryant exhorted his troops over the TBS (Talk Between Ships) radio: "Get on them, men! Get on them! They are raising hell with the men on the beach, and we can't have any more of that. We must stop it!"

The U.S.S. *Shubrick* saw a German officer spotting for guns on a crest and fired a four-gun salute; the German simply disappeared. Between 10:00 a.m. and 10:30 a.m. the U.S.S. *Frankford* cruised up and down the beach, firing at German targets, and subsequently, action on the beach increased.

At the seawall on Omaha Beach, courage, leadership, initiative, and training overcame the natural incli-nation to hunker down. As German mortar fire landed around them, Col. George Taylor said: "Two kinds of people are staying on this beach, the dead and those who are going to die—now let's get the hell out of here!"

The Assistant Division Commander of the 29th Division, Brig. Gen. Norman "Dutch" Cota, led a group of men through the wire surrounding the beach and onto the bluffs and then returned to the beach to do it over again. Lt. John Spaulding's boat made it safely onto the beach, and one of his sergeants found a trail in defilade, which the squad took to get around the German trenches. They used grenades and M-1s to clear the

ABOVE, LEFT: A machine-gun crew of men from mixed units provides covering fire behind Omaha Beach on D-Day. Some of these men are from the 2nd Ranger Battalion, which suffered 50-66 percent casualties in the initial assault waves. Six ammunition boxes are visible on the right-hand side of the photograph, attesting to the level of fighting. ABOVE, RIGHT: A dead soldier lies at the base of a beach obstacle he was attempting to blow up. Crossed rifles were a tribute to a fallen comrade. BELOW: Such beach obstacles as these steel I-beams offered some protection from rifle and machine-gun fire. Infantrymen were able to catch their breath for a few moments, but German artillery and mortar fire made it impossible to remain on the beach without being killed or wounded.

trenches and made it to the bluffs behind the beach. All over Omaha the process was repeated as junior officers and noncommissioned officers led small groups of men up the draws and behind the Germans. By 10:30 a.m. there were pockets of Americans on the crest.

On the right flank of Omaha, American Rangers (highly trained elite troops modeled on the British Commandos) scaled the cliffs at Pointe-du-Hoc, intending to destroy casemented 155mm guns, which were capable of sinking ships in the invasion fleet. Rangers fired grappling hooks like mortars up to the plateau, but the Germans threw them down, so the Rangers put fuse cords on the grappling hooks, lit the fuses, and then fired them; the Germans left them alone. Other Rangers climbed to the top of the cliffs on expanding ladders provided by the London Fire Brigade. On the plateau they found a German deception—the casements contained telephone poles, not guns. Sgt. Leonard Lomell

and Sgt. Jack Kuhn moved farther inland, found the 155s, and disabled them with thermite grenades placed in the breech blocks. Sgt. Frank Rupinski's patrol blew up the battery's ammunition dump. What had started as potential disaster turned into a very important victory for the Allies.

LEFT, TOP: The turret of a German Mk-IV tank, with its characteristic short-barreled 75mm gun, served as a beach defense at Omaha Beach. Obsolete as a fighting tank by 1944, its relatively short range, 500 yards (914m), was still effective against troops and landing craft. LEFT, BOTTOM: Moments after Capt. Herman Wall, U.S. Army Signal Corps, took this photograph around noon on Omaha Beach, he was struck by artillery fragments. Evacuated three hours later, he lost part of his leg and received the Distinguished Service Cross.

An aerial view of the landings shows numerous craft and a few LSTs approaching the beach while streams of vehicles proceed off the beach and a German bunker position burns at the upper center.

Gold Beach

Gold Beach was the geographical center of the Normandy beachhead. The landing of the British 50th Division went according to plan. Lt. Pat Blamey commanded a Sherman carrying a 25-pound (87.6mm) gun. After a landing he called "a pushover," crediting the RAF and the Royal Navy for its ease, Blamey drove off the beach and entered Asnelles, where he and his crew stopped to brew some tea.

Seaman Ronald Seaborne was feeling seasick by the time he got to shore. With a name like Seaborne, he was made a forward observer for the HMS *Belfast*, which provided fire support for Gold Beach. Unable to raise (contact via radio) the *Belfast*, Seaborne pressed inland to join his party and ran into three Germans who he thought would kill him, but they turned out to be Russians who wanted to surrender; Seaborne pointed them toward the beach. Passing through a church graveyard, he was fired at by a German sniper; he fired back until he got the German with a ricochet: the Englishman's last bullet. When the sniper turned out to be a boy, Seaborne felt sicker than he had in the landing craft.

Juno Beach

Farther to the east, the first wave of the Canadian 3rd Division experienced terrible casualties on Juno Beach, but by the end of the day the Canadians were farther inland than men on any other beachhead. Their opponent was the 716th Division—made up of men who were under eighteen, over thirty-five, or veterans of third-degree frostbite. For transportation, the 716th had bicycles and horses, which suited the third of them who were Georgians and Russians. About 400 of these "Germans" were about to try to stop 2,400 Canadians in the first wave.

Unlike Dieppe in 1942, where Canadians had no battleship support, this time the Royal Navy's cruisers and battleships began firing at 6:00 A.M., destroyers at 6:19 A.M., LCTs with tanks and 25-pound guns at 7:10 A.M., and LCTs with rockets after that. The smoke and haze were so thick that the gunners could not even see

the bombardment. Later it was calculated that only 14 percent of all bunkers were destroyed, while the vacation homes that had been turned into fortified positions were imploded; they simply fell in on themselves.

Sapper Josh Honan was attached to the Regina Rifle Regiment for demolition work. He and his major jumped from their landing craft and started removing detonators from mines attached to beach obstacles sticking up above the water. When the tide rose so that he could no longer reach the mines, he swam ashore and entered Berières-sur-Mer. People greeted the Canadians with roses, and the town barber gave Honan a shave.

Sword Beach

At the extreme eastern end of the invasion, on Sword Beach, the British 3rd Infantry Division got off the

French troops of the 2nd French Armored Division land on Utah Beach on August 1, 1944. They went on to fight most of the war with Lt. Gen. George S. Patton's Third U.S. Army except when they took part in the liberation of Paris while attached to the First U.S. Army.

Two young German soldiers captured in the first week of the Allied invasion undergo the identification process, in which intelligence found out what units each prisoner belonged to so as to enable the Allies to figure out how many enemy units they were facing, or the order of battle, prior to being shipped to England on the *Warspite*. Note the improvised desk of ration boxes.

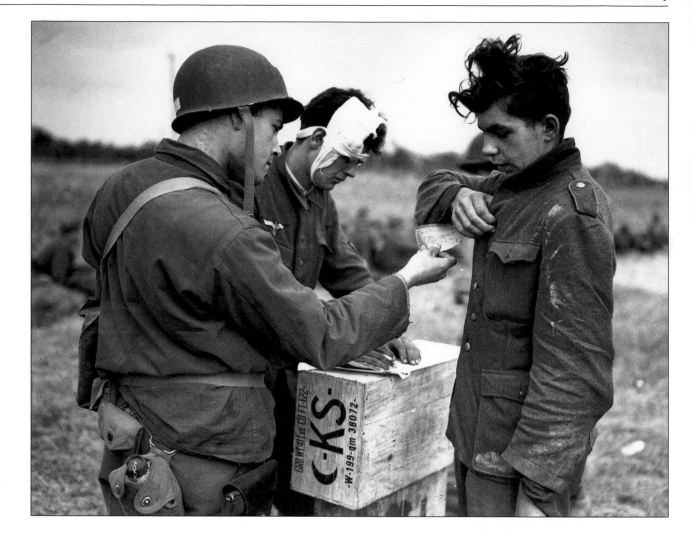

beach in less than an hour. The British 6th Airborne had silenced the Merville battery during the night, and the Villerville battery fought it out with HMS *Warspite* rather than fire at more vulnerable beach targets.

Wing Commander L.C. Glover was the RAF spotter on the *Warspite*, and after he gave the fire coordinates, his aircraft experienced a drastic bouncing. Glover said, "I saw two enormous objects moving rapidly away from me toward the shore . . . I had flown at right angles through the slipstream of *Warspite*'s two ranging 15-inch [38cm] 'bricks.'" Glover could see the huge shells (the "bricks") as they fell, and one knocked out the target. Two other Allied pilots made the same mistake, but they were never found.

The British also dealt effectively with smaller targets thanks to Maj. Kenneth Ferguson of the British 3rd

Division, who commanded a squadron of British Major General Sir Percy Hobart's specially redesigned tanks, also known as Hobart's funnies, in the first wave on Sword. After a German antitank gun fired at his tank, a Sherman bridge-carrier, one of Hobart's funnies, put the gun out of action by putting its bridge on the gun. Ferguson's funnies blew gaps in the wire and sand dunes and dropped bridges over the seawall, allowing the bulldozers and fascines (bundles of bound sticks) carriers to fill in the antitank ditches. To clear mines, Ferguson's flail tanks drove off the beach and up the dunes, turned around, and flailed back to below the high-water line.

French commandos also landed on Sword Beach, and when their LCI (Landing Craft Infantry) struck an obstacle, three of them jumped from their craft and raced through the water for the honor of being the first to return to France. One, Pvt. Robert Piauge, came from Ouistreham, about three miles (5km) away; but he came in third. Hit by a mortar, given a morphine injection, and expected to die, the twenty-one-year-old Piauge started to cry—from the joy of being in France. Piauge survived with twenty-two metal fragments in his body.

Pvt. Piauge was not the only local resident on Sword Beach. A French Red Cross nurse, Jacqueline Noel, came to the beach to recover the bathing suit that her twin sister had given her on their birthday. Once a week residents were allowed to swim at the beach, and Noel had left her suit in a bathhouse; her sister had been killed by a British bombing raid on Caen two weeks earlier. Wearing her Red Cross armband got her through the German lines, but the British would not let her return, so she tended the wounded.

Also landing on Sword Beach were Brigadier Lord Lovat's commandos. Lovat's piper, Bill Millin, played "Bonnie Dundee" during the landing. Among the

LEFT: Maj. Gen. Sir Percy Hobart's "funnies" were tanks modified for special tasks. This flail tank was an AVRE (Armored Vehicle Royal Engineers) designed to clear paths through minefields quickly at little risk to the tank and its crew.

ABOVE: Prime Minister Winston Churchill (left) talks with Field Marshal Sir Alan Brooke, CIGS, on the open bridge of a British destroyer bound for Normandy on June 12, 1944. Throughout the campaign in northwest Europe, Churchill kept in close touch with his field commander, Gen. Montgomery.

RIGHT: British troops land on
Gold Beach on June 6, 1944.
The picture shows both metal
and wooden beach obstacles.
OPPOSITE: Infantrymen of the
British 3rd Division on Sword
Beach carry their wounded
and move to higher ground.
Some men crouch while
others walk upright, passing
dead comrades.

commandos was the famous British actor Maj. David Niven. Later on D-Day the commandos linked up with British Maj. John Howard's glider men at the Orne and Caen Canal bridges while Sgt. Millin played the pipes. Before they pushed inland, the commandos left Howard two Germans who had been captured without their pants; one commando said that they belonged to the "German Pantsoff Division."

At 4:00 P.M. the German 21st Panzer Division finally counterattacked the British on Sword. The Germans had been driving around since 9:00 a.m. Originally the 21st was supposed to attack paratroops east of the Orne River, but it was rerouted through Caen to attack the gap between the British and the Canadian beaches. It ran into a fusillade of antitank guns and rocket-firing RAF Typhoons, and although it opened a gap that extended to the beach itself, it was quickly turned back.

The First Step

Hitler's Atlantic Wall had not done as well as the French Maginot Line. The Atlantic Wall had taken four years to build, and the Allies took it in less than an hour at Utah Beach, just within an hour at Sword and Gold Beaches, within two hours at Juno Beach, and in less than five hours at Omaha Beach.

All over Normandy Allied soldiers knew they had accomplished the first step of a long journey; few could have guessed what awful fighting awaited them over the next six weeks—the battle of the hedgerows.

On the night of D-Day thousands of men would have understood Sgt. John Ellery of the 1st Division— the "Big Red One"—when he said: "I had made it off the beach and reached the high ground. . . . I had walked in the company of very brave men."

Chapter 2

German Defeat in France

ALL OVER NORMANDY, AS THE SUN SET ON JUNE 6, TIRED AND HUNGRY MEN stopped to consider the magnitude of their accomplishment. The headquarters of Maj. Gen. Matthew Ridgway's 82nd Division reported: "Short 60 percent infantry, 90 percent artillery, combat efficiency excellent." It must have been, because later that night the 82nd halted a German counterattack within 400 yards (350m) of Ridgway's headquarters.

By nightfall on D-Day, only the British and Canadians from Gold and Juno Beaches were linked at Cruelly. The D-Day planners had wanted to link up all the beachheads, but had been overreaching in their goals. Distances between the invasion beachheads were three miles (5km) between Juno and Sword, almost seven miles (11km) between Omaha and Gold, and eleven miles (18km) between Omaha and Utah. It took the next six days for all the beachheads to be linked up to form a contiguous lodgement area.

The Allies had to continually expand the beachhead to gain the space required by their follow-up divisions as well as airfields and supply dumps. At his pre-invasion briefing on May 15, Gen. Montgomery said that the Allies needed "to gain space rapidly, and peg out claims well inland." Montgomery pointed out that the Allies would have to gain a line running south of Caen through Falaise to Argentan and then west through Vire to Granville on the Bay of Biscay.

Northwest Caen had been a D-Day objective, and the city proper was a British objective for D+5, or June 11, but the Germans hung onto its vital roadnet for another five weeks.

LEFT: In one of the singular moments of the war, on August 29, 1944, the 28th Infantry Division, under Brig. Gen. Norman D. Cota, marched down the Champs Elysées in Paris. Whereas Germans marched in conquest here in June 1940, Americans marched in liberation. Actually this parade served as a tactical maneuver that facilitated the division's movement through the city to the northern suburbs and into combat.

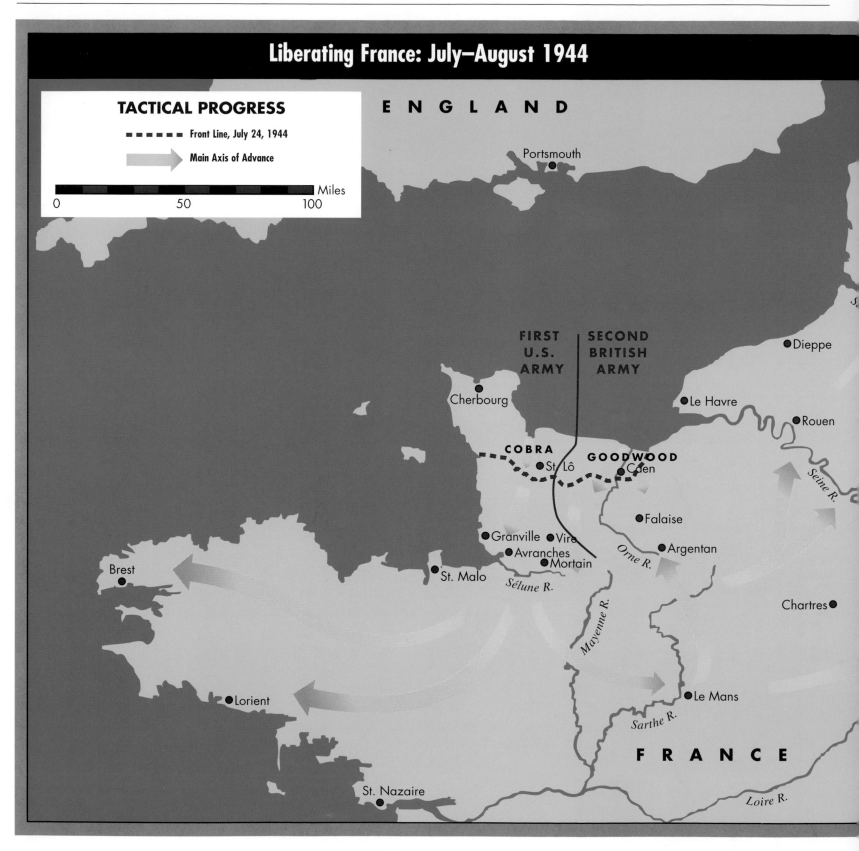

Liberating France: July–August 1944

TACTICAL PROGRESS

- - - - - Front Line, July 24, 1944

➡ Main Axis of Advance

Miles

0   50   100

ENGLAND

Portsmouth

FIRST U.S. ARMY

SECOND BRITISH ARMY

Dieppe

Cherbourg

Le Havre

Rouen

COBRA

St Lô

GOODWOOD

Coen

Falaise

Granville

Vire

Argentan

Avranches

Mortain

Orne R.

St. Malo

Sélune R.

Mayenne R.

Chartres

Brest

Le Mans

Lorient

Sarthe R.

FRANCE

St. Nazaire

Loire R.

LEFT: The Allied breakthrough at St. Lô led to Gen. Patton's breakout at Avranches and resumption of open warfare into Brittany and beyond. Instead of retreating across the Seine as German generals urged, Hitler ordered an armored counterattack towards Avranches, which the Allies stopped at Mortain. Stubborn German resistance prolonged the campaign until August 19, with the closing of the Falaise-Argentan gap.

The Battle of the Hedgerows

In addition to fronts in Russia, Italy, and Yugoslavia, after June 6, Hitler had to deal with a front in France only 350 miles (560km) from the Ruhr; an Allied Blitzkrieg from there had the potential to reach the industrial heart of Germany. Prior to June 6, Hitler had said repeatedly, "If the invasion is not repulsed, the war is lost for us." Four days after the landings Hitler ordered the Seventh Army in Normandy: "Every man shall fight or fall where he stands."

Behind the Atlantic Wall the Germans initially had no prepared defenses. Fortunately for them, from Bayeux to the Bay of Biscay thousands of man-made hedgerows gave their name to the terrain, the bocage. For centuries Norman farmers had divided their fields by growing hedges, which every other year they cut back for firewood. Over time an average hedgerow grew four feet (1.2m) thick at its base, and its hedges grew from

Dukws, cranes, trucks, bulldozers, LCTs, and prefabricated buildings crowd Omaha Beach and the tidal flats. The naval and amphibious power of the Anglo-American coalition is clearly demonstrated.

RIGHT: British glider troops dig foxholes in an orchard near their glider behind Sword Beach in the first days of the invasions. BELOW: Five Americans have taken a hedgerow from the Germans, three of whom lie dead in the foreground. Fighting in the hedgerows was dangerous, frustrating, and interminable. Normandy was an infantry-man's battle, where vision was severely limited.

three to ten feet (.9–3m) high. The areas they contained varied in size from one to three football fields (100–300 square m).

Using the hedgerows, the Germans created defenses throughout Normandy. Germans sited tanks or antitank guns where they were nearly invisible and protected strong points with machine guns, mortars, and dug-in infantry. In the hedgerow battles around Caen, the Allies encountered Germans in prepared positions at depths up to ten miles (16km) from the city. The casualties incurred in taking these monotonous warrens fell almost entirely on the infantry, and most of them were caused by German mortars. In six weeks of combat the replacement rate in the U.S. 90th Division exceeded 100 percent for infantry-men and reached 150 percent for infantry officers.

American transport planes pulling gliders circle Les Forges, southwest of Utah Beach, on the morning of June 7, 1944. Several gliders have already landed in the center field to the left, bringing in the 325 Parachute Infantry Regiment as reinforcements. This photograph provides an aerial view of Normandy's hedgerows.

LEFT: Some 59,000 nurses served in the Army Nurse Corps in World War II, with more than 17,000 in the European theater. U.S. nurses of the 13th Field Hospital behind Omaha Beach take lunch in the field. The censor has deleted the unit insignia from their field jackets for security reasons.

RIGHT: This Mark-IV mounts a long-barreled 75mm gun, "bazooka skirts," and Zimmerit anti-magnetic coating; the tank was destroyed in the Falaise-Argentan gap. Note that steel plates are suspended from the turret and extra tank track wraps the hull, which was designed to set off bazooka rounds. The raised ridges seen on all flat surfaces were the Zimmerit paste that prevented infantry sticky bombs, such as Gammon grenades, from attaching to the tank.

LEFT, TOP: An American infantryman fires his bazooka from behind a hedgerow somewhere in Normandy on August 2, 1944. The American M-9 2.36 inch (60mm) anti-tank rocket launcher weighed 16 pounds (25.6kg) and could fire a 3.5 pound (5.6kg) rocket about 100 yards (183m). LEFT, BOTTOM: The 502nd Parachute Infantry of the 101st Airborne Division fight it out with Germans at a roadblock at Foucarville, northwest of Utah Beach, on June 10, 1944.

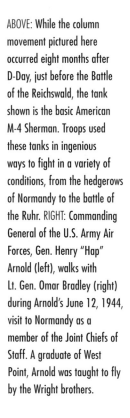

BELOW: An American bazooka team, a loader and operator, destroys a German tank in the first week of August. This remarkable photograph capturing the demise of a Panther tank and its crew demonstrates the range of the bazooka, the closeness of combat, and the bravery of these two-man bazooka teams.

ABOVE: While the column movement pictured here occurred eight months after D-Day, just before the Battle of the Reichswald, the tank shown is the basic American M-4 Sherman. Troops used these tanks in ingenious ways to fight in a variety of conditions, from the hedgerows of Normandy to the battle of the Ruhr. RIGHT: Commanding General of the U.S. Army Air Forces, Gen. Henry "Hap" Arnold (left), walks with Lt. Gen. Omar Bradley (right) during Arnold's June 12, 1944, visit to Normandy as a member of the Joint Chiefs of Staff. A graduate of West Point, Arnold was taught to fly by the Wright brothers.

Tanks

Throughout the battle of the hedgerows, German tanks proved far superior to their Anglo-American counterparts. German tank battalions were equipped primarily with Mk-IVs and Mk-Vs (Panthers), but heavy tank battalions had the Mk-VIs, the famed Tiger tanks. Carrying massive armor, the Panthers and Tigers weighed 45 and 54 tons (40.5, 48.6t) respectively, which was 50 and 80 percent more than the standard Allied tank. With nearly 4 inches (100mm) of frontal armor and powerful main guns, the Panthers and Tigers were virtually invulnerable to Allied tanks except from their flanks and rears.

The prototype Allied tank in Normandy was the American-made M-4 Sherman. Because of its relatively light armor and gasoline-powered engine, the Sherman tended to "brew up," or catch fire, when hit by antitank rounds. However, mechanical reliability and a power-traversing turret gave the Sherman an edge in maneuverability over the more cumbersome German tanks.

The British variant of the Sherman, known as the Firefly, mounted a 76.2mm, or 17-pound (8kg) gun, rather than the standard 75mm gun. Due to the Firefly's capacity to kill German Panthers and Tigers, its longer gun attracted attention on the battlefield, especially since only one in four British Shermans were Fireflies. The British also used Churchills and Cromwells in Normandy, but neither of their 75mm guns could take on German heavy tanks. Fortunately for the Allies, the constricted Normandy terrain limited most tank fights to between 150 and 400 yards (140–360m), which reduced the range advantage of German tank guns.

Mulberries

In the Bay of the Seine on June 7, the Allied navies started assembling the Mulberries, their prefabricated ports built in England. Capable of unloading 6,000 tons (5,400t) per day, the Mulberries had floating bombardons—huge, sausage-shaped breakwaters—to prevent a wave buildup. Closer to shore, the navies sank a blockship breakwater within which they assembled the Mulberries. Giant concrete caissons sunk to the ocean floor served as mounts for floating docks, capable of

Rhinos

Tanks could not bust through hedgerows—they had to climb over them; this meant exposing the tank's underbelly while its main gun pointed uselessly up in the air. Sgt. Curtis G. Culin, Jr., of the 102nd Cavalry Reconnaissance Squadron, 79th Division, got the idea of welding some of Rommel's beach obstacles to the front of a Sherman, allowing it to dig into the hedgerow like a giant pitchfork. A Sherman with Culin's teeth was known as a "Rhino," and it went through the hedgerows "as though they were pasteboard." By mid-July about 60 percent of U.S. Shermans had been turned into Rhino tanks, allowing the First U.S. Army to break through the hedgerows during Operation Cobra. The Allies thought up this solution to the problem of getting through the hedgerows in six weeks, while the Germans had been in the area for four years but had not bothered to add extra defenses to the naturally-growing barriers, having never realized that tanks might get through them.

The Germans had been in Normandy for four years prior to the Allied invasion, but it took the U.S. Army's "citizen soldiers" about six weeks to come up with an answer to the hedgerow in the form of "Rhino," which was fashioned from Rommel's beach obstacles. Sandbags were added protection against bullets and ricochets.

Behind Omaha Beach on June 10, 1944, this 90mm gun fires on German positions. Normally antiaircraft weapons, the 90mm guns were turned against infantry in the absence of a German aerial threat.

moving with the tides, and floating pontoon piers linked the docks to the beaches.

Unfortunately, a storm destroyed the American Mulberry set up at Omaha; its salvaged parts helped repair the less damaged British Mulberry at Arromanches. Fortunately for the sake of resupply, the Anglo-Americans learned that LSTs could be beached at low tide, unloaded, and refloated at high tide without breaking their backs on uneven beaches, a process known as "drying out." "Drying out" LSTs eliminated the need to ferry supplies, which was one of the functions that the Mulberries were to facilitate. The loss of the American Mulberry, however, increased the significance of capturing the port of Cherbourg.

The Krupp 88mm Antiaircraft Gun

The Tiger I, Mk-VI, mounted a Krupp 88mm antiaircraft gun with a muzzle velocity of 3,280 feet (1,000m) per second that could penetrate 4 ¾ inches (120mm) of armor at 100 yards (90m) and 4 inches (102mm) of armor at 1,000 yards (900m). Originally designed for the navy but adopted as an antiaircraft gun, the Krupp was first used as an antitank weapon in 1940 in France. Rommel then employed the Krupp to great effect in the desert of North Africa owing to its extreme range and accuracy. Commenting on the characteristic sound of its high-muzzle velocity, flat trajectory shells, Americans said they sounded like "UUULLLNEVER GOBACK to AlaBAM!" The diameter of the 88's high-velocity shell was more than a match for Allied tanks.

The word FLAK comes from the German word *Flugzeugabwehrkanone* (aircraft-defense-gun). Both Krupp and Rheinmettal, weapons maunfacturers, received contracts for 88mm guns which Krupp had developed. Beginning in 1941, Krupp production switched mainly to the tank and antitank guns while Rheinmettal eventually took over production of the antiaircraft variants.

The U.S. Mulberry artificial harbor floats near Omaha Beach on June 16, 1944, three days before it was ruined by a gale. Vehicles leave the concrete piers, which rest on the seabed, and drive ashore on the floating pontoon road bridge.

Maj. Gen. J. Lawton "Lightning Joe" Collins was perhaps the best American corps commander of World War II. He pushed hard on his division commanders and was the favorite of First Army Headquarters.

Cherbourg

Following the capture of Carentan at the base of the Cotentin Peninsula on June 12, Gen. Bradley ordered Maj. Gen. J. Lawton Collins's VII Corps across the Cotentin to the Bay of Biscay, to cut off the peninsula prior to his attack on Cherbourg. Known as "Lightning Joe," Collins had been a division commander on Guadalcanal and was regarded as the foremost corps commander of the First Army.

Collins designed an aerial bombardment of the German positions leading to Cherbourg using both the British and American tactical air forces as well as Bomber Command. The German commander at Cherbourg, Lt. Gen. Karl Wilhelm von Schleiben, refused a surrender ultimatum and held out until June 26. Other elements held out until June 29, which was long enough for the German navy to demolish the Cherbourg port complex so completely that Allied engineers did not clear the last obstacles until late September. By November, until the weather halted unloading on the Normandy beaches, 14,500 tons (13,050t) of supplies per day were being unloaded at Cherbourg—more than 70 percent over the original estimate of its capability.

General Montgomery and Caen

On the eastern flank of the lodgement area the Germans frustrated the Allied buildup by holding Caen. On the plains below Caen the terrain changed from hedgerows to rolling hills, far better tank country than the western flank. A British breakthrough from Caen to the Seine River would outflank the German line of supply and communication from Paris. Therefore, the Germans concentrated 80 percent of their armor in Normandy against the British on the eastern flank.

Gen. Montgomery faced contradictory challenges. As ground forces commander he had to steadily expand the beachhead to avoid a stalemate, but as 21st Army Group commander he was the ranking British officer on the continent and had to keep down British casualties. Before the invasion the War Office told him to expect a 35,000-man shortage in infantry replacements by

An American artillery crew fires a 105mm howitzer at a German position near Carentan on June 11, 1944. Most artillerymen suffered full or partial hearing loss from the war.

mid-summer. In July the War Office moved up the warning, pointing out that the level of casualties would soon necessitate breaking up an infantry division to provide individual infantry replacements.

To hold Caen while not weakening their Fifteenth Army in the Pas de Calais, the Germans reinforced Normandy with panzer units from Brittany and southern France. One of the first arrivals was Panzer Lehr, under Lt. Gen. Fritz Bayerlein, an elite tank demonstration division twice the size of Allied tank divisions. After inspecting Panzer Lehr, Gen. Heinz Guderian, the head of German armored forces, told Bayerlein, "With this division alone you will throw the Anglo-Americans back into the sea."

Fortunately the Allies had complete aerial superiority, and their fighter-bombers took a toll on German columns and headquarters personnel. Moving to his assembly point in Normandy cost Bayerlein five tanks, eighty half-tracks and self-propelled guns, and forty gasoline trucks. His troops called the road from Falaise to Beny-Bocage *Jabo-Rennstrecke*—"fighter-bomber race course." Ultra detected the headquarters of the German Panzer Group West, and RAF Typhoons destroyed it on June 10. The Germans buried seventeen officers, including their chief of staff and the entire operations section, in one of the bomb craters, over which they erected a huge oak cross with an eagle and a swastika.

Troops of the 101st Airborne Division move into the road junction town of Carentan on June 12, 1944. After repulsing a German counterattack on June 13, troops from Omaha and Utah Beaches linked up at Carentan, solidifying their beachheads in Normandy.

On June 13 Montgomery attempted to gain Caen by double-envelopment from the southwest and the east. On the southwest beyond Villers-Bocage a column from the British 7th Armored Division, the "Desert Rats," encountered SS Capt. Michael Wittman of the 1st SS Panzer's attached heavy tank battalion. Wittman, already renowned within the German army for his exploits in Russia, charged the British column in his Tiger, knocked out its lead vehicle, and drove its length, pumping rounds into the immobilized force. Returning to his base twice to fuel and rearm, Wittman, along with four other tanks, destroyed twenty-five tanks, fourteen trucks, and fourteen Bren gun carriers before a British antitank gun knocked out the Tigers. Wittman escaped this battle on foot, but his luck finally ran out in August when he was killed near Falaise—not before, however, he had knocked out 138 Russian and British tanks.

Meanwhile, to the east of Caen, the 51st Infantry Division could not wrest the steel works at Colombine from the 21st Panzer Division and pulled back. Montgomery's veteran divisions (the 7th Armored, the

ABOVE: A German sniper lies dead in a Cherbourg doorway. Capt. Earl Topley, who had just led his troops into the city, said this German had killed three of his men on June 27, 1944.
LEFT: Germans in fixed fortifications at Cherbourg meet their fate. The two American soldiers in the lower left have just set off a satchel charge to wipe out the bunker.

BELOW, RIGHT: St. Lô was an important communications center and was bombed continuously from D-Day until it fell on July 19, 1944. When St. Lô fell to the Americans, it had been nearly destroyed, and the French called it the City of Ruins. Only the towers of Our Lady's Church, to the left center, remained standing.

50th and 51st Divisions) were unaccustomed to conditions in Normandy and displayed some edginess. Having come through the desert, Sicily, and Italy, they were old soldiers and would not take the same risks that "green" divisions would. Habits acquired in the desert, like tank commanders riding with their upper bodies out of their turrets, were fatal in the hedgerows.

On June 26, while the Americans were taking Cherbourg, Montgomery launched Operation Epsom, which was a two-corps attack begun in bocage country about halfway between Villers-Bocage and Caen. By June 29 the British 11th Armored Division was on its objective, Hill 112, which dominated the terrain west of Caen and south of the Odon River. Despite repulsing counterattacks by the 9th and 10th SS Panzer Divisions (recent arrivals from the eastern front), the 11th Armored

was withdrawn from Hill 112 by Lt. Gen. Sir Miles Dempsey, British Second Army commander, who feared further counterattacks; with that decision, Epsom went from success to failure.

Meanwhile, the War Office's grim prediction was proving true. Second Army had lost 4,000 men killed and wounded in the last five days of the battle, half of them in the infantry; its total casualties since D-Day numbered 45,000.

The Toll on the Germans

On the German side of the hill it was grimmer still. The incessant infantry attacks, artillery barrages, bombing, and naval gunfire took their toll. Since D-Day the Germans had lost more than 2,300 officers and 94,000

The Assassination Attempt

Having lost his left eye, right hand, and the third and fourth fingers of his left hand in North Africa in 1943, Col. Count Klaus von Stauffenberg was posted to the army staff and often personally briefed Hitler. Convinced that Hitler was a genocidal maniac, the count became active in the plot to kill the dictator, and he nearly succeeded on July 20, 1944.

Called to Hitler's headquarters at Rastenburg in east Prussia on July 20, von Stauffenberg placed a briefcase carrying a bomb under Hitler's map table, excused himself to make a phone call, and left the room. Another officer, unawares, then repositioned the briefcase to the outside of the table's heavy oak support, which shielded Hitler from the eventual blast. When the plot was discovered, von Stauffenberg and several other officers were shot by firing squad; they were relatively lucky. Other plotters were arrested, tortured, hauled before the so-called People's Courts, humiliated, convicted, and executed by guillotine, hanging, firing squad, or in some cases by garroting with piano wire suspended from meat hooks.

enlisted men, while receiving only 6,000 replacements. The day after the British crossed the Odon River, Gen. Friedrich Dollmann, commander of the German Seventh Army, lost heart and poisoned himself. Dollmann's superiors, Rommel and von Rundstedt, were in Berchtesgaden where Hitler told them: "We must never allow mobile warfare to develop since the enemy surpasses us by far in mobility." They were to hold at all costs; Hitler expected German soldiers in Normandy to die harder.

Returning to his headquarters, von Rundstedt read a withdrawal plan from the commander of Panzer Group West, Gen. Leo Freiherr Geyr von Schweppenburg. Both the general and von Rundstedt agreed to withdraw their troops beyond naval gun range, and they forwarded the plan to Hitler's headquarters. Upon receiving the plan,

ABOVE: Field Marshal Günther von Kluge replaced Field Marshal von Rundstedt as Commander in Chief West but was unable to stem the Allied breakout in Normandy.

Rommel's End

In late July, Rommel was nearly killed when his command car was strafed near the village of Ste. Foy de Montgomery. While Rommel recovered from his wounds, the German secret police linked him to the plot to kill Hitler. Even though he was not directly involved, Rommel knew of the plot to kill Hitler and approved of it because of the course of the war.

On October 14 two generals from Berlin came to Rommel's home near Ulm and informed him of Hitler's ultimatum and Rommel's choices—commit suicide or face trial by the People's Court. Assured that his family would be safe, Rommel said good-bye to his wife and son and left with the officers, who gave him a poison capsule. The German public was informed that Hitler's favorite general had succumbed to his wounds.

Field Marshal Erwin Rommel was the epitome of the successful Blitzkrieg commander who always led from the front. This trait suited Rommel to division command but it exhausted him when he commanded a corps in Africa; he suffered a nervous and physical breakdown and had to return to a sanatorium in Europe to regain his health.

Caen, once William the Conqueror's capital city, was reduced to rubble by British strategic bombers as part of Gen. Montgomery's controversial Operations Epsom and Goodwood (both named after British racetracks). This photograph shows a bulldozer clearing a path through the rubble that was once people's homes.

Field Marshal Wilhelm Keitel, head of OKW (Oberkommando der Wehrmacht, High Command of the Armed Forces), called and asked, "What shall we do?" Von Rundstedt answered, "Make peace, you fools. What else can you do?"

Hitler relieved both von Geyr and von Rundstedt on July 2; Rommel said, "I will be next." Field Marshal Günther von Kluge arrived on July 3 to take von Rundstedt's place.

Operations Goodwood and Cobra

After Epsom failed, Gen. Montgomery agreed to two massive "carpet-bombing" attacks in mid-July. Planned by Dempsey and Bradley, and set to go off within a day of one another, Operations Goodwood and Cobra were designed to deepen the Allied lodgement in Normandy.

Goodwood was to outflank Caen from the east using three armored divisions to gain the vital Bourguébus Ridge seven miles (11km) to the southwest, while the Canadians completed the conquest of Caen south of the Orne River. On the western flank Cobra would see the First U.S. Army attack south from the road junction town of St. Lô, some ten miles (16km) from Coutances. However, recent rains had turned the bocage into a swamp and delayed First Army's drive toward St. Lô, so Gen. Bradley postponed Cobra.

When Operation Goodwood achieved its goal without breaking through to the enemy's rear on July 18, following a carpet bombing of 7,000 tons (6,300t) of bombs, Eisenhower wondered if the Allies could afford 1,000 tons (900t)of bombs for every mile gained. Goodwood expanded the lodgement by thirty square miles (78 square km), but at the cost of 5,000 casualties and 400 tanks, or 36 percent of the British tanks in France. SHAEF thought that Goodwood was an expensive failure because an earlier plan had mentioned Falaise as an objective, while the revised plan, which SHAEF never received, said that only armored cars were to venture as far south as Falaise. Allied air force generals, both U.S. and RAF, were disappointed with Montgomery because the lodgement's area was just one-fifth the size anticipated in the Overlord plan for

mid-July; this limited the air forces to seventeen airfields instead of the planned twenty-seven, and to half of their planned sixty-two squadrons. Additionally, the use of strategic bombers in tactical support of the ground troops always proved controversial because it contradicted air force doctrine of strategic bombing

Once the Americans had seized the vital road junction town of St. Lô on July 18, Bradley was ready to launch Cobra. His plan called for the U.S. Eighth Air Force to carpet bomb an area 6,000 yards (5,500m) long

The eight-day battle for St. Lô, fighting through the hedgerows, culminated in the city itself and cost more than 5,000 American casualties.

Gen. George S. Patton, Jr., shown in 1945 as a four-star general. Slapping two GIs in Sicily in 1943 cost Patton command of 12th Army Group, which went instead to Gen. Bradley. Operational conduct of the campaign would have differed had Patton been in charge rather than Bradley.

parallel to the St. Lô-Périers Road and 2,500 yards (2,300m) south of it. The infantry divisions of Collins's VII Corps would make the initial attack on July 25–26, followed up by reserves of two armored divisions and another infantry division. Bad weather in France forced Cobra's postponement on July 24 while bomb groups were in the air, and they bombed perpendicular to the St. Lô-Périers road through overcast skies, hitting the U.S. 30th Division and inflicting 150 casualties and twenty-five fatalities.

On July 25, 1,500 B-17s and B-24s, followed by fighter-bombers of the Ninth Tactical Air Force, dropped 3,400 tons (3,060t) of bombs, again flying perpendicular to the road. Unfortunately, the bombs fell within American lines again, wounding nearly 500 and killing 111. The Eighth Air Force had told Bradley that his parallel-bombing plan would have taken four hours to fly through the bomb zone, and they told him to back up 1,500 yards (1,400m), but Bradley had his ground units back up 800 yards (730m). Both Bradley and the Eighth Air Force were negligent.

Ernie Pyle, the GI's favorite war correspondent and an eyewitness, recalled men lying on the ground "like cartoons of people flattened by steamrollers." Among the dead was Lt. Gen. Leslie J. McNair, who had gone into a small building that took a direct hit. McNair was the highest-ranking American killed in Europe, and SHAEF kept his death a secret to protect its deception plan. Pyle was so disillusioned by Cobra that he returned to the United States following the liberation of Paris.

Gen. Bayerlein's Panzer Lehr took the brunt of Cobra's bombing, which killed 1,000 and wounded one third of its men in the target area. Immediately after the attack a staff officer from von Kluge's headquarters arrived with an order to hold the St. Lô-Périers road. Bayerlein was incredulous, and exaggerated slightly in his reply: "Out in front every one is holding out. . . . Not a single man is leaving his post. They are all lying silent in their foxholes for they are dead. You may report to the Field Marshal that the Panzer Lehr Division is annihilated."

Bradley's First Army faced eleven German divisions but only two panzer divisions. Initial progress on July 25 was slow. For 3,400 tons (3,060t) of bombs, the Americans moved about two miles (3km), but given their own friendly-fire casualties that was significant. Acting on intelligence that the Germans were stretched very thin, Collins intuitively ordered two of his reserve divisions into the battle on July 26, and they began to make rapid progress to the south and southwest. On July 28, along the Biscay coast, the VIII Corps belonging to Maj. Gen. Troy Middleton moved south in support of Collins's right flank.

First Army had grown so large that several of its corps transferred to the command of the Third U.S. Army, under Lt. Gen. George S. Patton, Jr. Unofficially supervising the VIII Corps beginning on July 28, Patton changed its attack plan, substituting two armored divisions, the 4th and 6th, in the place of two infantry divisions. Patton's substitution was a stroke of genius. On July 30 the 4th Armored entered Avranches. The next day, when the 4th Armored seized the Pontaubault bridge over the Sélune River, Patton had opened the gateway into Brittany.

The Americans had not only broken through the German lines south of St. Lô, they had broken out of the German lines at Avranches. None of the Allied generals at the time had expected this to occur, however. All thought that Cobra would expand the lodgement area, that the Germans would withdraw to a new line, and if everything worked to perfection, the Americans would be positioned to break into Brittany to capture its ports. Unexpectedly the Allies had entered the phase of mobile warfare that Hitler feared most.

The Falaise-Argentan Pocket

On August 2 Hitler ordered von Kluge to attack with four panzer divisions toward Avranches to cut off the corridor into Brittany and then to turn northeast to drive into First Army's flank.

Ultra alerted Bradley to the counterattack on the night of August 6, and the RAF and Ninth Tactical Air Force wreaked havoc on the German armored divisions caught in the open on August 7. The U.S. 30th Division was overrun by the 2nd SS Panzer Division, but the 30th held Hills 314 and 317 east of Mortain, spotting

Side roads leading from Falaise became charnel pits owing to Allied tactical air forces and artillery fire. This is what remains of one German column caught on the road. One German general was reminded of a Crusader's poem from the twelfth century, "Man, horse, and truck by the Lord were struck."

When French troops paused under the Arc de Triomphe to pray at the eternal flame on August 25, 1944, a German tank, parked in the Place de la Concorde at the other end of the Champs Elysées, fired upon them. The gunner on a French Sherman set his gun to 1,800 meters and destroyed the German tank with a single shot.

invited the Allies to trap his armor in Normandy. As the Canadians pushed down from the north, and the Americans from the west and the south, a pocket of Germans was trapped west of the road junctions of Falaise and Argentan.

On August 1 Bradley advanced to command of the U.S. 12th Army Group, with operational control of Patton's Third Army and his previous command, First Army, now under his former deputy, Lt. Gen. Courtney H. Hodges. Montgomery remained ground forces commander but in practice he coordinated operations with Bradley. By August 9 Patton had his divisions in Brittany on the outskirts of Brest, in LeMans, and, by August 13, in Argentan.

Controversy surrounds the closing of the Falaise-Argentan pocket in mid-August. Even though the German command was disorganized and the Allies had complete control of the air, the Germans were still able to hold open the gap between Falaise and Argentan, allowing men and equipment to get out. Patton wanted to move north of Argentan to meet the Canadians coming down from Falaise. In his best Anglophobic style, Patton told Bradley that his Third Army could "drive the British into the sea for another Dunkirk," meaning he wanted to attack north until he met the Canadians.

When the remark made its way to the British, they were not amused. However, it was Bradley, not Montgomery, who refused the move. More than risking an accidental encounter with the Canadian army, Bradley was clearly concerned about the power of the German panzers to prevent Patton from closing the gap. Bradley said, "I much preferred a solid shoulder at Argentan to a broken neck at Falaise." The Falaise-Argentan gap finally closed on August 19 when the Polish 1st Armored Division met the U.S. 90th Division at Chambois on the River Dives about seven miles (11km) east from Argentan.

There were probably 80,000 Germans inside the pocket, which was about one fourth of the Germans below the Seine. Most of the German army in Normandy would get away, maybe as many as 240,000, along with 28,000 vehicles and perhaps a hundred tanks. However, of the fifty organized, cohesive, divisions that had existed in June there were only ten in mid-August, and the

for artillery until relieved. Bradley used four divisions from Third and First Armies to stop the German counterattack.

Meanwhile, Montgomery ordered the Canadian First Army under Lt. Gen. H.D. Crerar, in its first independent operation, toward Falaise, and in concert with Bradley, sent Patton toward Argentan. By August 10 von Kluge, fearing encirclement, was able to convince Hitler to withdraw from Mortain, but by attacking toward Avranches rather than withdrawing to the east, Hitler

Falaise-Argentan pocket became the metaphor for the destruction of the German Seventh Army.

The damage wrought by rocket-firing RAF Typhoons and Spitfires was hideous; on the side road from Falaise to Trun, for example, German vehicles and dead stretched for over a mile. The Germans had suffered a second Stalingrad. The Allies had killed and wounded more than 200,000 Germans in Normandy and taken another 200,000 prisoner.

The Liberation

Less than a week later, on August 25, the 2nd French Armored Division took Paris under Lt. Gen. Philippe Leclerc. "Leclerc" was a pseudonym, meaning "the clerk," adopted by the Vicomte Jacques-Philippe de Hauteclocque to protect his family, who had remained in France in 1940 after he went to London following the French surrender.

Leclerc had fought in North Africa. His division landed in Normandy on July 29, 1944, and fought alongside Patton's Third Army. Eisenhower assigned Leclerc to liberate Paris following the rising of the French Forces of the Interior there on August 20. Luckily the military governor, Lt. Gen. Dietrich von Choltitz, disobeyed Hitler's orders to burn the city, but his troops put up a stiff fight against Leclerc's tanks.

On August 26 Leclerc received the German surrender of Paris not for SHAEF but in the name of the Provisional Government of the French Republic, for Gen. Charles de Gaulle, leader of the Free French and head of the Provisional Government. That afternoon Leclerc walked from the Arc de Triomphe down the Champs Elysées to the cathedral of Notre Dame behind de Gaulle and Gen. Koenig. Standing unmoved while machine-gun fire broke out in part of the cathedral, probably from anti-Gaullist communists, they heard mass and Te Deum. Paris was liberated.

ABOVE: Finally able to return to French soil, Lt. Gen. Philippe Leclerc strides up the beach to take part in the liberation of his country from the Germans. LEFT: Parisians jam the Champs Elysées to cheer the American 28th Infantry Division as it marches toward the Arc de Triomphe during the victory parade of August 29, 1944. Many of the men marching here would die in the Hürtgen forest in November of that year or at Bastogne during the initial German attack in December.

Chapter 3

The Race to the West Wall

SEPTEMBER 1, 1944, WAS THE FIRST DAY OF THE FIFTH YEAR OF THE WAR IN Europe. Lt. Gen. Brian Horrocks's 30 Corps, the vanguard of the British Second Army, marked the anniversary by chasing the Germans out of France. Moving seventy-five miles (120km) on September 3, the Guards Armored Division liberated Brussels to a tumultuous greeting from the overjoyed Belgians.

The next day the 11th Armored Division rolled into Antwerp, taking Europe's second largest port before the Germans could damage it. The British had covered 250 miles (400km) in six days. Alexander Clifford of London's *Daily Mail* accompanied the British tankers, reporting, "This mad chase is getting crazier by the hour. The war in the West no longer exists. . . . Our columns just press on and on behind an army whose only strength is desperation. The idea of what we are doing is deliriously exciting. The atmosphere is heady and intoxicating."

Clifford captured the sense of euphoria that swept the Allied camp in September when victory seemed down the next road. After the breakout in Normandy, landings in southern France, and the liberation of Paris, the Allies began a race for the Rhine and an assault on the Ruhr, which many Allied soldiers expected would lead to a complete German collapse in 1944.

LEFT: An eight-man squad of the 9th Infantry Division's 60th Infantry Regiment approaches the German border on September 9, 1944. The last man is carrying a .30 caliber Browning Automatic Rifle (BAR). Note that the Sherman tank still mounts its rhino beams from Normandy and also sports extra armored plates welded to the side of the tank and the turret for additional protection.

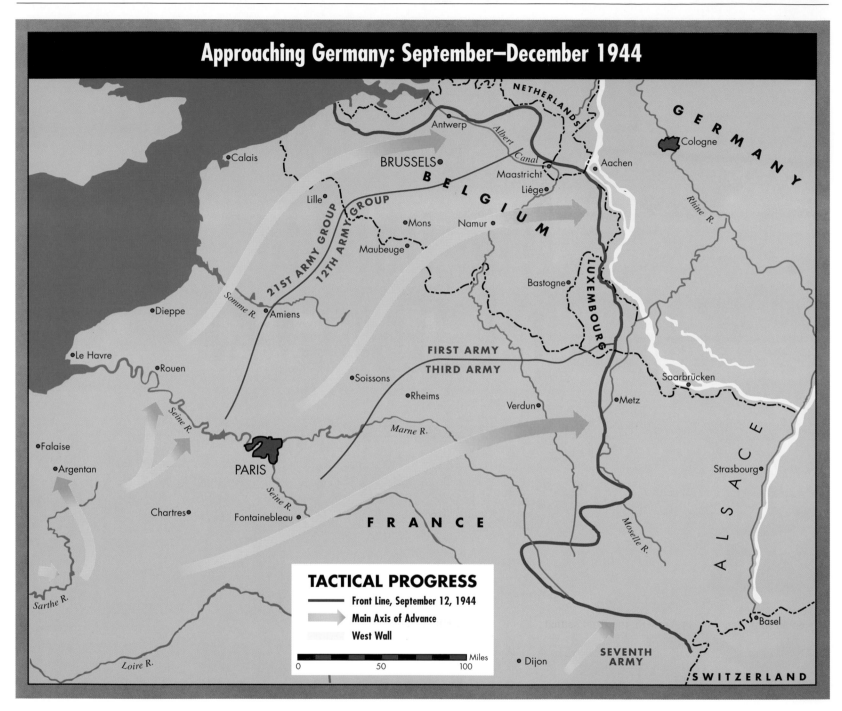

Approaching Germany: September–December 1944

TACTICAL PROGRESS

— Front Line, September 12, 1944

→ Main Axis of Advance

West Wall

0   50   100 Miles

September 1944 was a critical month for both the Anglo-Americans and the Germans. The German army in the west was critically short of tanks and men to hold both the Albert Canal and the West Wall. Consequently, rival plans developed in British and American army group headquarters to take advantage of Germany's weakness. Eisenhower opted for a broad-front strategy but backed Montgomery's single thrust toward Arnhem. However, the Germans stalemated the Anglo-American advance along this front for months and were able to prepare a strategic reserve for their last counteroffensive on the Western front.

Hitler's port strategy led to the deployment of this American 155mm gun (Long Tom) to Brest in late August 1944. Though they normally belonged to an army's artillery, these large guns were needed to oust the Germans from their concrete reinforced positions in the French port city.

Instead the German army in the west won the race to the protection afforded by the Albert Canal in Holland and the West Wall—a three-mile (5km) -wide defense made up of bunkers and pillboxes stretching along the western border of Germany. Key Allied command and strategic decisions in August affected operations in September, and when the Germans turned back the Allied airborne landings at Arnhem, the front settled down into another Normandy-like battle in which progress was measured by gains of yards rather than miles. Hitler played for time and got it; his twilight would last into 1945.

The Brittany Ports

At the end of July Hitler adopted a strategy to frustrate Allied logistics in order to gain six to ten weeks to restore the West Wall for the coming battle for Germany.

First, he declared all the Atlantic ports along the coast of France "fortresses," picked their commanders, and consigned their garrisons to death or capture. Next, Hitler ordered the systematic destruction of the French rail system—marshaling yards, bridges, locomotives, and machine shops. Reiterating his last man, last bullet mantra, in which he ordered his troops to fight to the last soldier, Hitler traded 200,000 Germans in Brittany, the Channel islands, and the Channel ports for time.

In the first week of August, the 6th Armored Division, under Maj. Gen. Robert W. Grow, raced more than 200 miles (320km) across Brittany, closing on Brest on August 7. Maj. Gen. Hermann B. Ramcke, a dedicated Nazi, had stiffened Brest's defense with the remaining members of his 2nd Parachute Division. Ramcke even retreated to a fort in the harbor where he could fire its last round before he surrendered on September 19. Bradley had to ration ammunition in the 12th Army Group to provide the half-million rounds needed to reduce Brest.

The Liberation of the Low Countries

In Belgium and Holland the joy of the people upon their liberation was spontaneous and heartfelt. One old widow wearing her husband's medals from World War I ran up to a British jeep in a convoy and pressed all she had of value, three cigarettes, into the hand of the driver telling him, "Je vous remercie, Tommy. Je vous remercie" ("I thank you, Tommy. I thank you").

In Holland the citizens slowed down the advance through the major cities by mobbing the troops. Weeks later Dutch people would yell "September 17" at Anglo-American troops in thanks for liberating part of their country in Operation Market-Garden (see pages 74–79).

The citizens of Belgium were universally grateful for their liberation at the hands of the Allies. Because they were a small country, they were less self-conscious than the French about their defeat in 1940. The Allied soldiers commented overwhelmingly at how much they were made to feel welcome by the Belgians. The crowds in the streets dancing and celebrating their liberation with an outpouring of gratitude even slowed down the progress of Allied columns.

The Overlord plan had intended to allocate Cherbourg to the British, while the Americans would use the Brittany ports of Brest, Lorient, St. Nazaire, and Quiberon Bay. During a one-month pause on the Seine, from D+90 (September 6) to D+120 (October 6), COMZ ("com zee"), the Communications Zone of European Theater of Operations U.S. Army, was to build bases in Brittany to support future operations. However, Hitler's port strategy ruined the Overlord logistics by forcing Eisenhower to cancel plans for Quiberon Bay and Brittany bases at Rennes.

During the six-week siege of Brest the front moved past Paris, into Belgium, Holland, Lorraine, and Germany. Cancellation of the Brittany ports plan meant that the British would not have exclusive use of Cherbourg, and the American supply operation would have to depend upon Omaha Beach and smaller Normandy ports. Furthermore, the Germans began a systematic dismantling of what was left of the French railroad system after the Transportation Plan, the bombing of the French rail system prior to D-Day by strategic bombers and fighter bombers.

The Pursuit Without Pause

As a result of Hitler's counterattack against Avranches, the German dictator let his armored divisions in for a crushing defeat, and when the German Seventh and Fifteenth Armies eventually pulled out, they were too weak to defend any line in northwest France. The Germans abandoned tons of equipment in an attempt to get to the safety of the West Wall in Germany and the Albert Canal in Holland. The Germans' headlong flight left Eisenhower with little choice on August 19 but to jump the Seine without pausing to build bases. At the time he still harbored hopes for Brest, but in another month he simply discarded what remained of the Allies' logistics plan.

As the Anglo-Americans raced for the West Wall, they daily increased the distance between the front and their bases in Normandy, while the Germans quickly fell back on their bases in Luxembourg, eastern France, and

Germany. Neither the British nor the Americans had sufficient trucks to supply their armies more than 250 miles (400km) from Bayeux and Cherbourg. To continue the pursuit, both Montgomery and Bradley grounded their heavy artillery in Normandy in order to employ the artillery's trucks to haul supplies to the armies. Montgomery grounded one corps west of the Seine for two weeks to use its trucks to support his other two corps, and he cut daily port discharge from 16,000 to 7,000 tons (14,400 to 6,930t) because his trucks were engaged in long-hauling to the front.

COMZ and the Red Ball Express

In August and September, there was a gas crisis at the front. The British discovered that 1,400 of their 3-ton (2.7t) "lorries" (trucks), along with their entire pool of replacement engines, suffered from defective piston

LEFT: These 4-5 ton (3.6-4.5t) tractor-trailers are part of the famed Red Ball Express, hauling 2,000 gallon (7.6 million l) semitrailers. The Red Ball Express was a direct result of the success of Hitler's port strategy, and despite herculean efforts, a gasoline shortage developed at the front, which in turn permitted the Germans to defend most of the West Wall before the Anglo-Americans could seize it. OPPOSITE: German resistance in Brest was over by September 18, 1944, but not before much of the city, such as this former German headquarters, was devastated by bombing and artillery.

rings; the loss of these trucks cost the British deliveries of 800 tons (720t) per day, enough to supply two divisions.

The Americans did not have enough truck companies to handle port clearance, depot hauling, and long-haul delivery on account of a decision made by COMZ in 1943. While planning the invasion, COMZ had reduced the Transportation Corps' recommendation of 240 truck companies for Overlord to 160, largely owing to difficulties in finding shipping space for truck companies. By using trucks of ten divisions grounded west of the Seine, as well as artillery, chemical, and antiaircraft units, and by employing the airlift of the IX Troop Carrier Command, SHAEF assembled the equivalent of the missing 80 truck companies. With the armored divisions moving faster than the airborne forces could plan operations, the Allies used the troop carrier aircraft, as well as heavy bombers, to carry gasoline, blood plasma, and new maps to the front. Furthermore, after capturing Paris, the Allies had to feed it, which took 4,000 tons (3,600t) per day, the equivalent of three days' worth of supplies for movement toward Germany.

Within a week of Eisenhower's decision to jump the Seine, COMZ began the Red Ball Express. The Red Ball Express operated on one-way roads to deliver gasoline to the front-line units; it ran around the clock and drove with lights at night, ignoring the German Air Force. More than 1,500 trucks delivered an average of 8,200 tons (7,380t) a day over a typical round-trip of 700 miles (1,120km). The round-trip to Patton's forces on the Moselle, for example, took three days at the authorized 25 mph (40kph). Demonstrating the law of diminishing returns, while delivering gasoline to the First and Third Armies, which used up 800,000 gallons (3 million L) a day, Red Ball used more than 300,000 gallons (1.1 million L) per day, about one day's supply for three armored divisions. The British equivalent delivery operation Red Lion delivered supplies to Montgomery during the Arnhem operation.

Closing down after eighty-one days, Red Ball had delivered more than 400,000 tons (360,000t) of supplies and gasoline, but the frantic process took its toll on men and machines. COMZ had collected the trucks for Red Ball's long-haul operations by cutting back on port discharge and inter-depot movement, which guaranteed that

This photograph captures the concentration of infantrymen fighting house-to-house in Brest in early September 1944. Squads often took corner houses and dynamited their way down the street by blowing consecutive walls between the houses. Notice the fixed bayonet on the crouching infantryman across the street; it testifies to the presence of Germans as the soldier wearing it expects to have to stab someone with it in hand-to-hand combat.

Allied warships pound the German garrison of Toulon on August 25, 1944, in support of the French attack on the Mediterranean port city, east of Marseilles. Within days, the French had captured nearly the entire German garrison of 18,000 men, greatly adding to the success of Operation Dragoon, the invasion of southern France.

the ports were soon choked with supplies and ships were backed up in harbors or anchored in England waiting to unload in France.

The Invasion of Southern France

Operation Dragoon (originally Anvil) took place along the French Riviera on August 15, 1944. Its chief critic, Prime Minister Churchill, watched from the destroyer HMS *Kimberley* as the U.S. Seventh Army landed

86,000 men, 12,000 vehicles, and 46,000 (41,400t) tons of supplies. Churchill complained to his wife that the fighter-bombers and navy silenced the German guns so quickly that it was almost boring.

By August 28 the First French Army, under Gen. Jean de Lattre de Tassigny, had captured the ports of Marseilles and Toulon; these two ports accounted for 40 percent of all American imports in October. Also in the first two weeks, the French First and the Seventh U.S. Armies, under Lt. Gen. Alexander Patch, captured 57,000 Germans at the cost of 4,000 French and 2,700

American casualties. Hitler had realized that the junction of the two separate invasion forces would cut off all German elements in southwestern France, so on August 17 he had allowed German forces to evacuate southern France.

By September 11, near Dijon, French patrols made contact with Americans from Patton's Third Army, and by September 15, the 12th Army Group joined up with the 6th Army Group under Lt. Gen. Jacob L. Devers, commanding the Seventh U.S. Army and the First French Army. When Devers's army group passed from control of the Mediterranean Theater of Operations to the European Theater of Operations, Eisenhower commanded three army groups along a front from the North Sea to the Swiss border.

Eisenhower's Broad-Front Strategy

As a coalition commander, Eisenhower had to see that the forces of each member of the coalition played a role in Germany's defeat. In May 1944 Eisenhower approved the so-called broad-front strategy, drawn up by SHAEF planners, which proposed two axes of advance on the Ruhr, one north and one south of the Ardennes plateau.

The Allies assumed that capturing the Ruhr, the industrial area that accounted for two thirds of Germany's steel and more than half of its coal, would end the war. SHAEF's planners split the front because the partially forested Ardennes plateau contained practically no east-west roads. North of the Ardennes the advance would be on the line of Amiens-Maubeuge-Liege-Ruhr, with the Aachen gap offering the best avenue of advance to the Rhine. South of the Ardennes the advance would be on the roadnet of Verdun-Metz-Saarbrücken-Frankfurt. Eisenhower envisioned Montgomery commanding the main advance in the north and Bradley directing the secondary advance in the south. SHAEF also intended to make use of the historic Belfort Gap leading to Germany from Alsace. Assuming their troops would be more mobile than the Germans, SHAEF planners wanted to threaten all the historic approaches simultaneously in order to keep the Germans guessing as to which avenue contained the main attack.

Eisenhower's assumption of the ground command in September stemmed from American political considerations. After an article in *The New York Times* asked on August 17 why Americans in Normandy were still under British command when American forces constituted the majority of both the troops and the casualties, Secretary of War Henry L. Stimson and Gen. Marshall cabled Eisenhower to "assume command of the American contingent" as soon as possible. At the next Anglo-American conference, which included Montgomery's Chief of Staff Maj. Gen. Sir Francis de Guingand, Eisenhower announced that he would assume the ground forces command on September 1.

Montgomery's Strategic and Command Alternatives

To Montgomery the broad-front strategy meant that all units would be constantly fighting, there would be no strategic reserve, and neither thrust would be strong enough to exploit a breakthrough.

Days before, Montgomery had broken up the British 59th Infantry Division to provide infantry replacements. To prevent further cannibalization, his 21st Army Group required an infusion of American troops to see it through the campaign. Montgomery proposed his single-thrust plan to Bradley, suggesting that east of the Seine their two army groups approach the Ruhr north of the Ardennes "as a solid mass of some forty divisions which would be so strong that it need fear nothing." Bradley, however, was interested in his own thrust toward the Saar and Frankfurt.

Unable to enlist Bradley's support, Montgomery had to face Eisenhower alone. He told the supreme commander that simultaneous attacks would fail because there were only enough supplies for one concentrated thrust, and that he, Montgomery, should remain ground forces commander or, if American public opinion would not accept that, he offered to serve under Bradley. Montgomery believed that as supreme commander Eisenhower ought to "sit on a very lofty perch" and not "descend into the land battle."

Lt. Gen. Omar Bradley, 12th U.S. Army Group commander, awards the Bronze Star to Lt. Gen. Courtney H. Hodges, commander of the First U.S. Army. The First Army was first to land in Normandy, first to cross the Seine, first into Paris, first into Belgium, first into Germany, first to cross the Rhine, and first to link up with the Russians.

Marching in double file, soldiers of the First U.S. Army cross the German frontier to converge on the fortress city of Aachen, located near the borders of Holland and Belgium. Aachen was the first major German city to fall to the Allies.

However, Eisenhower reasoned that just as American opinion would not stand for Montgomery commanding American troops given the two-to-one disparity in divisions, neither would British opinion stand for Bradley's promotion over Montgomery and Montgomery's apparent demotion. Neither was Montgomery planning to give up 21st Army Group command for the ground forces command, and Eisenhower told Montgomery that unlike the battle for Normandy the front was too large for him to do both simultaneously, that is, command 21st Army Group and the Allied ground forces.

On September 1, 1944, Eisenhower assumed the ground forces command at his so-called forward headquarters at Jullouville, five miles (8km) south of Granville, on the Bay of St. Malo, 175 miles (280km) from Paris and some 300 miles (480km) from the front. At Jullouville Eisenhower was farther from the front than he had been at SHAEF's headquarters in Portsmouth, England.

On the same day, Bradley's 12th Army Group passed from command of Montgomery's 21st Army Group to direct command of SHAEF. To allay the pain of diminished command, Prime Minister Churchill had King George VI promote Montgomery to field marshal in recognition of his victory in Normandy.

Optimism in the West

While recuperating from the July 20 assassination attempt, which injured one arm, broke his eardrums, and left the Führer unsteady on his feet, Hitler replaced Field Marshal von Kluge, von Rundstedt's successor in the west, with Field Marshal Wilhelm Model, because he suspected von Kluge of attempting to surrender to the Allies during the Falaise-Argentan gap battle. Von Kluge committed suicide on his way back to Germany on August 18 rather than face the People's Court over his knowledge of the assassination attempt.

In Rumania five days later a coup toppled the pro-Nazi dictatorship, and the Rumanians quickly sued for peace with the Russians and declared war on Germany. At the end of the month the Russians captured the

SHAEF and the August Command Flap

Eisenhower tried to keep secret the fact that General Bradley's 12th Army Group was operational after August 1, 1944, in Normandy. Montgomery had been in command of First U.S. Army, and Bradley's promotion was seen as Montgomery's demotion by many in Britain. SHAEF made matters worse when the story leaked out and SHAEF denied what all the war correspondents knew was true.

Montgomery actually "coordinated" command with Bradley, but when the news reached England, along with SHAEF's denial, there was a furor in the British press. The Philip Zec cartoon in the *Daily Mirror* and its accompanying editorial on August 17, 1944, demanding that SHAEF apologize to Montgomery for its incompetent handling of the affair, was an example of hurt feelings in Britain. The resulting press flap made Eisenhower sensitive to Montgomery's role over the next few weeks and stopped Eisenhower from making Bradley the ground forces commander over Montgomery, as that would have been seen as a further demotion of the esteemed British general.

During the German Ardennes offensive, Eisenhower placed Montgomery in operational command of two American armies. Here Montgomery is pictured with his four army commanders, from left to right: Dempsey, British Second Army; Hodges, First U.S. Army; Montgomery; Simpson, Ninth U.S. Army; Crerar, Canadian First Army.

Ploesti oil complex in Rumania, Germany's largest natural source of oil. The Bulgarians, too, asked the Soviets for peace terms. And in the first week of September the Finns accepted Russian peace terms.

There was no fighting the resultant optimism in the Allied camp. In his mid-August press conference Eisenhower warned publicly against excessive optimism, pointing to German "fanaticism" in Brest, and its raising new formations; furthermore, Eisenhower predicted (correctly, as it turned out) that Hitler would never surrender and would probably kill himself at the last moment. No one paid any attention, however, least of all SHAEF's G-2 (Intelligence) Section, which by the end of the month was predicting an imminent German collapse. "The August battles have done it and the enemy in the West has had it. Two and a half months of bitter fighting have brought the end of the war in Europe within sight, almost within reach."

Capt. Harry Butcher, U.S.N.R. (U.S. Naval Reserve), Eisenhower's press aide, had Brig. Gen. T. J. Betts, the deputy G-2, frighten the war correspondents about the Siegfried Line, the Americans' term for the West Wall. After handing the correspondents Butcher's line, one of them asked whether we would get through the Siegfried Line. "Why of course," Betts assured them, "we'll go right through it."

The Albert Canal, Antwerp, and the Scheldt Estuary

When the British took Brussels and Antwerp, British intelligence noted that German units on the Albert Canal consisted of the 719th Division ("composed mainly of elderly gentlemen . . . who had never heard a shot fired in anger"), a battalion of Dutch SS trainees, and Luftwaffe troops.

By the fifth anniversary of the war, Wehrmacht losses totaled 3.75 million men. On September 2 Hitler called for twenty-five new Volksgrenadier divisions for deployment between October and December. Only 8,000 men strong, Volksgrenadier divisions came equipped with the new 1944 machine pistols. Trained to fight from prepared positions, these divisions also had a larger stock of antitank weapons. The Germans found the additional manpower by drafting hundreds of thousands of men from factory jobs, using slave laborers from concentration camps, conscripting foreign nationals, and for the first time, hiring German women to take their places. By lowering the draft age, stripping the navy and air force of all but essential personnel, and reducing training, the Germans raised thirty-five divisions of dubious quality. Hitler also raised ten new panzer battalions, each based around forty Panther tanks.

Ironically, while Montgomery's armor occupied the second largest port in Europe, the British commander ordered a halt because his supplies were coming from Bayeux, over 300 miles (480km) to the rear. With the potential answer to every Allied supply problem staring them in the face in the form of Antwerp's more than 25 miles of docks, warehouses, and quays, Horrocks, Dempsey, Montgomery, and Eisenhower all overlooked the obvious. Opening Antwerp to ship traffic would have solved all their supply problems, but it required opening the Scheldt Estuary. However, the commanders were not

considering the Scheldt Estuary—they were thinking about the Rhine. They thought the Germans were beaten, and this misconception made them consider operations before logistics, a mistake that lengthened the war.

Adm. Sir Bertram Ramsay, the Allied expeditionary force naval commander, warned both SHAEF and the 21st Army Group on September 3 that Antwerp, some 60 miles (96km) inland on the Scheldt Estuary, would be "highly vulnerable to mining and blocking." Unheeded, Ramsay's warning became a prediction. An identical warning was received via Ultra days later relaying that Hitler intended to hold the Scheldt Estuary at Walcheren Island and at the Breskens pocket, west of Antwerp, but still no one at SHAEF or 21st Army Group paid the slightest notice.

Hitler recalled Gen. von Rundstedt on September 5 to provide stability in the west. In the process Hitler demoted Field Marshal Model to command of Army Group B. Along the Albert Canal from Antwerp to the Maastricht appendage, Hitler installed the father of the German airborne, Luftwaffe Gen. Kurt Student, as commander of the First Parachute Army. Soon paratroops from all over Germany were rushing to the Albert Canal.

Meanwhile, the commander of the 85th Attack Infantry Division, Gen. Kurt Chill, on his own initiative, paused on the Albert Canal, gathering remnants of several divisions and stragglers from all three services. With this hodgepodge, renamed Kampfgruppe Chill (Battlegroup Chill), he turned back the first assaults on the Albert Canal on September 6 and helped limit the British bridgehead at Beeringen. When the British assault on the canal was renewed on September 8, Allied gains were no longer so rapid.

Montgomery had assumed that the First Canadian Army could clear the Scheldt and open Antwerp as it cleared the Channel ports, but capturing Le Havre, Boulogne, and Calais took the British 49th and 51st Infantry Divisions and the Canadian 3rd Division from September 10 through October 1. Dunkirk held out for the duration, as did Lorient and St. Nazaire in Brittany; Montgomery invested Dunkirk with a Czech Armored Brigade. The British gained several ports close to their line of communication, which greatly eased their logistical problems relative to the Americans.

ABOVE: **General Kurt Student was a German Air Force officer who helped create the German airborne forces. Student was largely or partly responsible for their victory in Crete, the rescue of Mussolini, and the defense of the Albert Canal and the West Wall. As a reward for his work, Hitler gave Student command of Army Group H in the Netherlands.** LEFT: **A slit trench changes hands in the Roer area as infantrymen of the Ninth U.S. Army clear a German trench in late November 1944. This was dangerous work because bodies were often booby-trapped with mines or hand grenades that went off when a body was moved.**

RIGHT: Following an occupation of nearly three years, this German prisoner of war receives a soccer-style send off from a French woman in Toulon, France, in late August 1944, much to the amusement of troops (military police) riding in the jeep. BELOW: German coastal defense guns of Fort Lamalgue in Toulon, France, were damaged by Allied naval gunfire in late August 1944 during the Franco-American attack on the Mediterranean coastal port.

Unfortunately Montgomery would not devote his army group's main effort to clearing the Scheldt Estuary until mid-October, by which time the Germans had mined and blocked the estuary and flooded Walcheren Island. The Canadians and the Royal Marines finally took Walcheren Island and the South Beveland Peninsula with amphibious vehicles on November 4, but mine-sweeping operations required three weeks. The first ship did not sail into Antwerp Harbor until November 28, more than twelve weeks after Horrocks had taken the port.

Operation Market-Garden

On September 10, Eisenhower approved Montgomery's plan for Operation Market-Garden, a combined airborne-armored assault from the Dutch border north to the Zuider Zee.

The plan involved an armored movement by 30 Corps (called Garden) of nearly 100 miles (160km) from the Meuse-Escaut Canal through Holland to the Zuider Zee, connecting with the airborne divisions (called Market), which would seize bridges over the Maas (Meuse) River, the Waal (Rhine), and the Neder Rijn (Lower Rhine), plus several canals. The roadnet ran Eindhoven-Son-Veghel-Uden-Grave-Nijmegen-Arnhem. The plan promised to cut off the German Fifteenth Army in western Holland, to outflank the West Wall near Nijmegen, and to threaten the Ruhr's northern flank. The major drawback was that it failed to address the German Fifteenth Army on both banks of the Scheldt Estuary's approach to Antwerp.

The First Allied Airborne Army under the command of Lt. Gen. Lewis Brereton, an Army Air Forces officer, would direct Market. Brereton had no airborne experience and quickly sided with the Troop Carrier Command's limiting its planes and pilots to one mission per day. The limitation meant that the three airborne divisions would land over several days, and none would have their full complement of men and weapons from the outset. Subsequently, Market was not big enough to land on both sides of each bridge, and delays in seizing the Nijmegen bridge over the Waal proved critical. By doing this, Brereton doomed Market to failure. If the planes were too precious to lose, then they could have continued to fly gasoline to Patton, who had come to a halt on the Moselle for lack of fuel that had been diverted to Market-Garden.

Brereton's deputy and commander of the I Airborne Corps was Lt. Gen. Frederick A.M. "Boy" Browning of the Grenadier Guards. Browning was the father of the British airborne. At a briefing at Montgomery's headquarters, Browning asked the field marshal, "How long do you think we shall have to hold the bridge at Arnhem?" When he was told two days, Browning said, "We can hold it for four. But, sir, I think we might be going a bridge too far."

The largest concentration of transport aircraft in history, over 1,500 planes and nearly 500 gliders, dropped components of three divisions with great accuracy around midday on Sunday, September 17. The British 1st Airborne landed near Model's Army Group B Headquarters as Model was having a glass of wine. He evacuated his headquarters and alerted the 9th and 10th SS Panzer Divisions; they had just completed an exercise in antiairborne assault tactics. Owing to the urban sprawl of Arnhem and the RAF's fear of flak near its objectives, the 1st Airborne landed more than six miles (10km) from the Antwerp bridges; furthermore, their armored jeeps did not arrive.

The division commander, Maj. Gen. Robert E. Urquhart, had no previous airborne experience, was prone to air sickness, and during the early hours of the battle, was cut off from his battalions while he hid in a local Dutch home to evade German patrols.

Men of the 8th Infantry Regiment of the 4th Division move to contact with the enemy but are pinned down by German small arms. They are fighting to capture the road junction in the Belgian town of Libin on September 7, 1944. Battles took place for the control of roadnets; whoever held the roads controlled the entire area.

RIGHT: The perfect weather of the first day of drops, September 17, 1944, for Operation Market-Garden did not continue long enough for the three scheduled drops to occur on three consecutive days, greatly impacting upon ground operations. BELOW: A Sherman tank of the Guards Armored Division crosses the Wilhelmina Canal on September 18, 1944, at Best, courtesy of the 101st Airborne Division's 506th Parachute Infantry Regiment. The cobble-stone street is part of the road nicknamed Hell's Highway, which the Germans cut several times during the operation.

Lt. Col. John Frost marched into Arnhem and took the north end of the Arnhem road bridge; the Germans drove back all attempts to take the south end with 20mm guns. Frost's men held Arnhem for four days. By the time the Germans took it back, more than half the paratroops were dead or wounded, and they were out of food and nearly out of ammunition. SS panzer grenadiers gave brandy and chocolate to the British survivors and congratulated them on the way they had fought.

The Irish Guards led 30 Corps' ground attack from the jump-off point on the Meuse-Escaut Canal. Zero hour was at 2:00 P.M. on Sunday, September 17, and by the day's end the Irish Guards had reached Valkenswaard, six miles (10km) short of their objective in Eindhoven. As the British settled down for the night the Germans brought up fresh men and equipment. Advancing on a raised causeway above the Dutch polders, the line of attack was as narrow as the cleared tracks through the minefields at El Alamein in the Egyptian desert in October 1942. As in Egypt, the camouflaged 88mm guns and German tanks took a heavy toll on the British armor.

As soon as the 101st Airborne landed they began fighting off German attacks on the highway from Eindhoven to Arnhem, dubbed "Hell's

Highway" by the Americans. On September 19 the Germans attacked Lt. Edward L. Wierzbowski's rein-forced company of paratroopers at the Wilhelmina Canal at Best, wounding Pvt. Joe E. Mann in both arms. His arms bandaged and tied in slings, Mann sat in a trench with six other wounded while the Germans threw hand grenades. Soldiers tossed out two, but Mann felt a third hit, and he covered it with his back. Mann lived long enough to tell Wierzbowski, "My back is gone"; he received the Medal of Honor posthumously. With only three unwounded men left, Wierzbowski surrendered. Later in the day Germans counterattacked the 101st at Schijndel, but the paratroopers received unexpected, and much needed, armored assistance in the form of a crippled British Sherman commanded by Sgt. James "Paddy" McCrory. Having dropped out of the first day's advance because his tank could only make five miles per hour (8kph), McCrory simply drove straight into the Germans.

That afternoon an Allied counterattack of 101st paratroopers and glider infantry supported by British tanks battled the remnants of the German 59th Division of the Fifteenth Army. By late afternoon they had routed the Germans, killing more than 300 and capturing 1,400.

Lt. Wierzbowski and his men reappeared, having talked a German aid station into surrendering.

The battles for Hell's Highway continued until September 26, when the Germans pulled out after cutting the highway twice and stopping all deliveries to the six divisions north of Veghel. Maj. Gen. Maxwell Taylor, the commander of the 101st Airborne, personally directed a 57mm antitank gun against a German armored counterattack on the floating pontoon Bailey bridge at Son. Taylor said that the attack reminded him of the Old West, when Indians would attack an isolated army garrison.

By the morning of Tuesday, D+2, the British had a Bailey bridge across the Wilhelmina Canal at Eindhoven. The Grenadier Guards crossed it at 6:15 A.M. and two hours later linked up with the 82nd Airborne in Grave. The German 10th SS Panzer Division was waiting with its 88mm antitank guns at the traffic circle below the Nijmegen highway bridge. Maj. Gen. James

A British 17 pounder (76.2mm) antitank gun crew prepares their weapon to protect the road bridge at Nijmegen, Holland, during Operation Market-Garden. The commander of the gun is wearing an American helmet. The German ability to hold this bridge, the largest of its kind in Europe, destroyed the Market-Garden timetable.

RIGHT: Little was left standing except the bridge over the Waal (Rhine) River following the battle for the road bridge at Nijmegen. The British jumped off from Nijmegen to begin their attack on the Reichswald in February, 1945. OPPOSITE: These lucky few were among the survivors of the British 1st Airborne Division that were evacuated across the Neder Rijn (Lower Rhine) in the closing hours of Market-Garden. Most are survivors from the battle west of Arnhem at Oosterbeek. Unfortunately, their 1st Airborne Division never fought again as a complete unit.

Gavin, the commander of the 82nd Airborne, had a plan to cross the Waal (Rhine) in boats, but the boats were down Hell's Highway at the rear of the British column. The Luftwaffe attacked the column in Eindhoven in its largest single raid of the campaign, killing 1,000 Dutch civilians in addition to British troops. By the time the boats arrived, there were just twenty-six of them instead of the promised thirty-three, and it was D+3.

While British and American troops battled for approaches to both road and railroad bridges, Maj. Julian Cook's battalion rowed across the 400-yard (350m) Waal. Germans on the opposite bank raked the boats with mortar and machine-gun fire. With twenty yards (18m) to go, Pvt. Joseph Jedlicka, a machine gunner, fell overboard into eight feet (2.5m) of water

wearing bandoliers and carrying ammunition boxes. Calmly holding his breath, Jedlicka walked the remaining distance on the river bottom. When Cook's men arrived on the north bank, they rushed the high ground without stopping. Watching the action from the south bank, Gen. Browning said to Gen. Horrocks, "I have never seen a more gallant action."

British tanks raced across the highway bridge while Cook's men killed the Germans on the bridge from the northern end. By the time Sgt. Peter Robinson of the Grenadier Guard's troop of tanks took the bridge, there were 267 Germans lying dead on it, and 30 Corps was eleven miles (18km) from Arnhem; its artillery could range the Germans surrounding the British 1st Airborne at Oosterbeek. On the next day, September 21, D+4, the

Germans captured Frost's band and retook the north end of Arnhem bridge. With the bridge once again in their hands, the Germans could put increased pressure on Nijmegen and points south because they no longer had to ferry tanks and troops on pontoon bridges over the Neder Rijn.

The British 43rd Infantry reached Driel, the ferry site on the Neder Rijn, and contacted elements of the Polish airborne on Friday, D+5, but the remaining pocket of the 1st Airborne was still surrounded in Oosterbeek. Finally, on the night of September 25–26, the last survivors of the British 1st Airborne Division evacuated across the river. Over 6,000 remained north of the river as prisoners, 1,400 were dead, and only 2,400 made it back.

The British 1st Airborne never fought again; it had been a magnificent failure, but a failure nevertheless. With the German stand on the Neder Rijn, the so-called German "Miracle of the West" was complete.

Hitler's fortress strategy had gained him the time that he needed to man the West Wall, raise new formations, create a panzer reserve, and plan the last German counteroffensive in the west. Stalemate settled in on the front, and Arnhem Annie, the German equivalent of Tokyo Rose, broadcast to the Anglo-Americans: "You can listen to our music, but you can't walk in our streets."

The West Wall

Germany's West Wall ran from the Dutch border near Nijmegen, south to Saarbrücken, then east to Karlsruhe, where it ran along the east bank of the Rhine down to the Swiss border at Basel.

Built between 1936 and 1938, the West Wall consisted of more than 3,000 pillboxes, bunkers, and command posts connected to defend Germany. Dr. Fritz Todt, the builder of the autobahn, the well-known German highway, directed its construction, and he designed it to follow ground features and fit in with rivers and lakes. Wherever there were large open spaces, Todt sowed rows of "dragon's teeth" to trap tanks and channel attacks to low ground. Built to an average depth of three miles (5km), the West Wall consumed one third of the annual German cement production. Its pillboxes were overgrown and obsolete by 1944, stripped of their 37mm antitank guns, and its gun ports were too small for modern 75mm and 88mm guns.

In 1944 the Germans planted mines, dug in tanks and 88mm guns, and brought up Volksgrenadier formations armed with four times the number of machine guns as an American rifle company; it became a daunting task to attack through a chain of mutually supporting West Wall pillboxes. The Allies called the wall the Siegfried Line after the famous Siegfriedstellung, the Siegfried fortress of the Meuse-Argonne forest, of World War I, which the Germans named after Siegfried, a mythical Teutonic warrior.

Seventeen soldiers of the 3rd Armored Division ride an M-4 Sherman tank-dozer through an opening in the dragon's teeth of the West Wall near Rötgen, the first German city captured by the First U.S. Army in mid-September 1944. Dragon's teeth were always present in flat open country and adjacent to roads in order to prevent tank attack.

Chapter 4

The Battle of the Bulge

ON DECEMBER 12, 1944, AT GEN. VON RUNDSTEDT'S HEADQUARTERS, HITLER BRIEFED HIS GENERALS on the offensive that they would launch in four days. For their audience with the Führer they had surrendered their personal sidearms and briefcases; while Hitler spoke, armed SS guards stood behind every chair. Hitler explained the offensive in Wagnerian terms:

> *Never in the history of the world have there been coalitions like that of our enemies . . . with such divergent aims. . . . Ultra-capitalist states on the one hand; ultra-Marxist states on the other. . . . If we can deliver a few more blows, then at any moment this artificially bolstered common front may collapse with a gigantic clap of thunder. . . . We must allow no moment to pass without showing the enemy that . . . he can never reckon on a capitulation. Never!*

The last great German offensive of the war in the west struck the First U.S. Army on Saturday, December 16, 1944, on a 60-mile (96km) front of the Ardennes plateau where the Belgian, Luxembourg, and German borders come together, from Monschau to Echternach. Twenty German divisions with a quarter of a million men and nearly 1,000 tanks smashed into all or parts of six American divisions numbering about 83,000 men. Nine days later the Germans came within three miles (5km) of the Meuse near Dinant, nearly 70 miles (112km) from their start lines.

LEFT: By January 4, 1945, the 75th Infantry Division's 290th Infantry Regiment had reinforced the 3rd Armored Division near Amonines, Belgium. The soldier at the right carries the M3 "grease gun," which was a cheaply made .45 caliber submachine gun prone to jams and rumored to have cost $8.00 to manufacture.

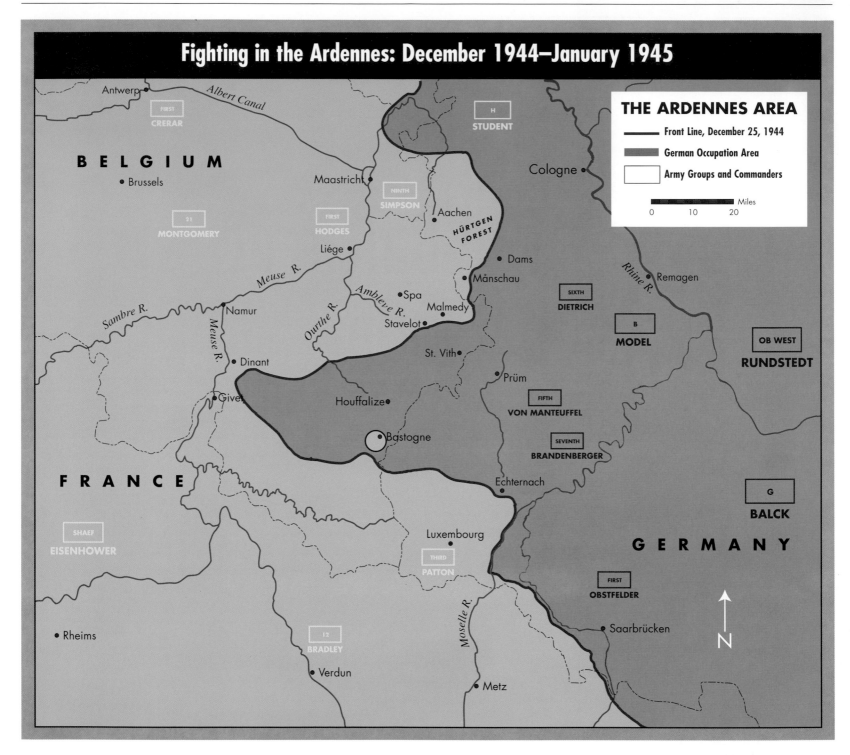

Fighting in the Ardennes: December 1944–January 1945

THE ARDENNES AREA

Front Line, December 25, 1944

German Occupation Area

Army Groups and Commanders

Miles
0   10   20

Antwerp

Albert Canal

FIRST
CRERAR

H
STUDENT

BELGIUM

Brussels

Maastricht

NINTH
SIMPSON

Cologne

Aachen

FIRST
HODGES

HÜRTGEN
FOREST

21
MONTGOMERY

Liége

Dams

Meuse R.

Månschau

Remagen

Rhine R.

Sambre R.

Namur

Ourthe R.

Ambleve R.

Spa

Malmedy

SIXTH
DIETRICH

Meuse R.

Stavelot

B
MODEL

OB WEST
RUNDSTEDT

Dinant

St. Vith

Givet

Houffalize

Prüm

FIFTH
VON MANTEUFFEL

Bastogne

SEVENTH
BRANDENBERGER

FRANCE

Echternach

G
BALCK

SHAEF
EISENHOWER

Luxembourg

GERMANY

THIRD
PATTON

FIRST
OBSTFELDER

Moselle R.

Rheims

12
BRADLEY

Saarbrücken

N

Verdun

Metz

The Germans achieved complete surprise in their counteroffensive in the Ardennes, which began on December 16, 1944. Eventually two United States divisions were rendered ineffective and never fought again as full divisions. Ironically, the initial debacle for the United States grew out of Eisenhower's broad-front strategy, which stretched out his forces along the Ardennes plateau and thus invited the German attack. However, since the Allies destroyed Germany's strategic reserves, the battle sped the end of the war.

A squad from the 82nd Airborne follows a Sherman through the snow in early January 1945. The horse, which is carrying bedrolls and a rifle, was probably captured from the Germans or borrowed from local civilians. German artillery was largely horse-drawn in the battle of the Ardennes and contributed to the Germans' logistical and transportation difficulties.

Initially the Anglo-American press called it the "von Rundstedt offensive," but the shape of the salient soon gave the attack its name: the Battle of the Bulge. Even though the Germans had moved through the Ardennes in 1914 and in 1940, Hitler still surprised the overconfident Allies.

Wacht am Rhein

The idea for an Ardennes attack came to Hitler in August while he was recovering from the recent assassination attempt, and planning began in September. Hitler reasoned that the twenty-five new Volksgrenadier divisions, ten panzer brigades, and 800 new tanks, mostly Panthers and the 75-ton (67.5t) Royal Tigers, stood to change the course of the war in the west against the relatively small Anglo-American forces, while reserves of

that size would have no impact on the thousand-mile (1600km) eastern front.

Demonstrating great craft, the Germans concentrated their offensive forces behind Cologne and the Saar, so that these panzer reserves appeared ready to counterattack the twin Allied offensives against the Roer River dams in the north and the Saar in the south. Even Hitler's original code name, *Wacht am Rhein* ("Watch on the Rhine"), would have confused both Germans or Anglo-Americans as to its true purpose.

In early December Hitler adopted another code name, which described his weather assumptions, *Herbstnebel* ("Autumn Fog"). To nullify Allied air power, Hitler needed ten consecutive days of bad weather, which would allow his forces to cross the Meuse, turn northeast, and retake Antwerp. Recapturing Antwerp would split the seam between British and American army groups. At best a German victory of this

Vehicles of the U.S. 87th Infantry Division move up near Wallerode, Belgium, about 2 1/4 miles (3.6km) from St. Vith, on January 30, 1945. Snow on secondary roads throughout the Ardennes made two-way traffic difficult and slowed attacks and counterattacks.

magnitude would lead to a negotiated settlement. At a minimum Germany would be free for some months to turn its entire might against the Soviet Union. To ensure utmost secrecy Hitler forbade any telephone, telegraph, or wireless mention of the plan and order of battle; any officer divulging this information faced death.

Hitler's plan stunned his generals. Initially von Rundstedt hoped that Hitler would settle for an attack out of the Ardennes against Aachen, but the Führer turned that idea down because it offered no likelihood of changing the war. In the final plan SS general Josef "Sepp" Dietrich's Sixth Panzer Army, with nine divisions, four of them armored, would be the main point of the attack. A World War I veteran and a Nazi Party member, Dietrich had joined the SS and commanded Hitler's personal bodyguard. Fifth Panzer Army's seven divisions, three of them panzers, all commanded by Gen. Hasso von Manteuffel, would guard Dietrich's left flank and cross the Meuse between Dinant and Namur on their way to Antwerp. Gen. Erich Brandenberger, the commander of the German Seventh Army, with four infantry divisions, was to protect von Manteuffel's southern flank.

The War of Attrition

When Hitler concocted his counteroffensive, he had no way of knowing that Eisenhower's broad-front strategy would play into his hands. Bradley's 12th Army Group had attempted to reach the Roer River in November and was preparing to gain the line of the Saar River in the south when Hitler struck.

To provide troops for offensives north and south of the Ardennes, Bradley had allowed First U.S. Army to hold the Ardennes with 70,000 men. In mid-1943 Secretary of War Stimson and Gen. Marshall had limited the U.S. Army to ninety divisions, with 14,000 men each, a tactic called the "90-Division Gamble." Stimson feared that the U.S. Army would be too small as a result but compromised because of the manpower needs of the other armed services and America's war industries. The broad-front strategy combined with the 90-Division Gamble to produce November 1944's war of attrition,

which in turn led to a serious replacement crisis in the U.S. Army.

By December most American divisions needed a rest. Eventually some sixty-eight U.S. divisions served in the European and Mediterranean theaters, but owing to the ninety-division limitation and the exigencies of a two-front war, American divisions seldom rotated out of combat as did German and British units. The odds of combat eventually caught up with an American rifleman, and he went home wounded or dead. Troops hoped for the "million-dollar wound," which would be bad enough to send them home but would not cost an arm or a leg, or worse.

A World War II American infantry division had twenty-seven rifle companies of 160 men, totaling 5,200 men in a division of 14,000. Of the 350,000 men in a typical American army, fewer than one of every seven soldiers closed with the enemy on the front line; some of the other six fought as machine gunners, artillerymen, engineers, or tankers, but the majority were support troops. Prior to Overlord, the U.S. Army estimated annual casualties at 70 percent, but in practice they were 85 percent; moreover, infantry rifle platoons experienced 90 percent losses. Only 70 percent of their replacements were riflemen, however. So by December 15, the 12th Army Group was short 17,000 riflemen among its thirty-one divisions. Nevertheless, Eisenhower believed that the assumptions behind his broad-front strategy justified battles of attrition.

The Hürtgen Forest Offensive

Throughout November 1944 the First U.S. Army launched an offensive through the Hürtgen forest southeast of Aachen. Gen. Hodges had feared a German counterattack from the Hürtgen as a result of his combat experience in the Meuse-Argonne in World War I, tacit recognition that the American army was refighting World War I. First Army's failure to recognize that no Allied army downstream from the Roer River dams near Schmidt could cross the river until the First took them marks the Hürtgen as the low point of American generalship during the campaign.

SS Gen. Josef ("Sepp") Dietrich, Nazi Party member, Hitler crony, and butcher by trade, spoke of his mission in the Ardennes: "All I had to do was to cross a river, capture Brussels and then go on and take the port of Antwerp."

ABOVE: Because the Sixth Panzer Army had been turned back at Elsenborn Ridge, the locus of the attack shifted to Gen. Hasso von Manteuffel's Fifth Panzer Army. From a distinguished Prussian military family, Manteuffel had persuaded Hitler to cut the preparatory artillery on December 16, 1944, from three hours to forty-five minutes on the grounds that it would insure surprise.

RIGHT: Troops of the 2nd Infantry Division withdrew from Rocherath-Krinkelt to Elsenborn Ridge on December 19, 1944. The 2nd Infantry Division and the 99th Infantry Division had already dented the attack of the Sixth Panzer Army in the northern half of the Ardennes. These men are crouching to avoid artillery fire on Elsenborn Ridge.

The Body Count of Autumn 1944

After the war Eisenhower wrote: "During this period we took as a general guide the principle that operations, except those areas where we had some specific and vital objective, such as in the case of the Roer dams, were profitable to us only where the daily calculations showed that enemy losses were double our own."

SHAEF G-2 noted that the Germans could raise about twelve divisions a month and could refit five. The constant Allied attacks destroyed three quarters of a German division per day, or about twenty per month. New German divisions entered battle with about six-weeks' training. Given this deadly exchange Eisenhower believed that the German front would soon crack.

This captured German photograph shows Germans looting American bodies. The German on the right is lacing up boots removed from the dead American on the left. The censor has whitened out the signpost for security reasons.

For ten weeks the battle raged over hills and valleys topped by 100-foot (30m) fir trees, where sunlight never pierced a forest floor littered with mines, decaying logs, and bodies. When German shells exploded among the tops of the fir trees, GIs would squat and cover their heads, thus lessening chances of being hit by splinters. Germans employed the infamous "Bouncing Betty" mine, which popped up, exploded above the knee, and emasculated a man.

First Army lost 24,000, killed, wounded, captured, or missing, and another 9,000 developed trench foot (a painful foot disorder resulting from exposure to cold or wet) or pneumonia. Six divisions suffered average losses of 25 percent, but none suffered more than the 28th Infantry Division, which lost more than 6,000 men and then went to the Ardennes for rest and refit.

The Ardennes Offensive Begins

At 5:30 A.M. Saturday morning, December 16, the German offensive began with a forty-five-minute artillery barrage. Attacking out of the night and fog, the Germans achieved complete surprise, and because of the short bombardment both Bradley and Hodges were confused by the intent of the initial attack. On the northern shoulder of the German breakthrough, the American 2nd and 99th Divisions held the high ground of the Elsenborn Ridge, which compressed Sixth Panzer's movement and forced it farther west in order to turn north for the Meuse.

The V Corps of Maj. Gen. Leonard Gerow held the Monschau-Butgenbach sector with the 2nd and 99th Infantry Divisions; it would become the northern

ABOVE: Lt. Gen. Courtney H. Hodges is shown here as a major general and Chief of Infantry. He became a lieutenant five years after he flunked out of West Point. Hodges served in World War I, won the Distinguished Service Cross, and commanded First Army from August 1, 1944, until the end of the war in Europe. Exhausted and in poor health during December 1944, he came close to being replaced by Joseph Collins.
RIGHT: A house burns in St. Vith, which was the key road junction town in the northern half of the Ardennes. Because Bastogne was surrounded and held out while St. Vith was taken by the Germans, the heroics of American troops at St. Vith have unfortunately been overlooked by the American public.

shoulder of the Bulge. Maj. Gen. Troy Middleton's VIII Corps ran southward through Germany, Belgium, and Luxembourg. The 14th Cavalry Group guarded the Losheim gap, the traditional invasion route from Germany into Belgium. The 106th Infantry Division entered combat four days before the German counter-offensive began, occupied about fifteen miles (24km) of German territory, and was less than ten miles (16km) east of the important road junction town of St. Vith. South of the 106th the battered 28th Infantry Division held a front of twenty-eight miles (45km) along Highway N7, "Skyline Drive," which paralleled the German border. The 9th Armored Division's front ran to Bollendorf, where it joined the 4th Infantry Division, which was also resting after its experience in the Hürtgen. The latter's front ran seven miles (11km) to Dickweiler.

Five German soldiers move through a ditch following an ambush on an American column. This picture was most likely taken on the morning of December 16, 1944.

The Guerrilla War of Lt. Eric Fisher Wood, Jr.

Lt. Eric Fisher Wood, Jr., of the 106th Division's field artillery was the last officer to pull out through Schönberg, eight miles (13km) east of St. Vith. None of Wood's unit got through the German roadblocks, but the men saw Wood, who played football for Valley Forge Military Academy and Princeton University, disappear into the forest.

Soon Wood began a guerrilla war with men he collected in the Ommer Wald between the Schönberg-St. Vith road and the village of Meyerode. Nazi general Dietrich made his headquarters in the village, and the villagers reported that he complained about "these Ami criminals and scoundrels" who shot German supply troops. Villagers found Wood's body on January 23, 1945, surrounded by seven dead Germans; all had been dead for an estimated ten days. Wood's body still bore his papers and 4,000 Belgian francs, proof that no surviving German had found it because soldiers routinely searched corpses for money.

The Belgians erected a cross where Wood had died, which his father, a general on the SHAEF staff, replaced with a monument. Eric Fisher Wood, Jr., received posthumously every medal for heroism except the Medal of Honor. The Medal of Honor requires two witnesses for corroboration, which of course was impossible in Wood's case.

ABOVE: Lt. Gen. Omar Bradley claimed in his memoirs that he had taken a "calculated risk" in holding the Ardennes with so few troops. In fact, he located his headquarters in Luxembourg to be close to Patton's upcoming Saar Offensive, scheduled for December 19, 1944. Bradley's mammoth headquarters diary first mentions a "calculated risk" on December 23, 1944, one week after the battle began. RIGHT: An American M10 tank-destroyer moves through the snow in the Ardennes. Undergunned and underarmored, with an open turret, it was the brainchild of Lt. Gen. Leslie J. McNair, chief of Army Ground Forces, who decided that American tanks would not fight German tanks, American tank-destroyers would. McNair's decision led to a doctrinal mutation that proved too lightly armed to fight tanks and was dangerous to its crews.

South of the 99th Division, the German Fifth Army's spearheads broke through, surrounded, and bypassed the green 106th. Great confusion led Maj. Gen. Allan Jones to keep his regiments in place when Gen. Middleton expected them to pull back. Several days later the 422nd and 423rd Regiments failed to get through German lines and surrendered. The capitulation of nearly 7,000 men was the low point of the American war effort in northwest Europe.

Pvt. Stanley Wojtusik of the 106th became a prisoner of war and marched off under armed guard toward Germany. Over the next four days Wojtusik ate only a single raw potato and endured temperatures around zero degrees (-18°C). Inside Germany one of his buddies could not keep up so Wojtusik carried him the last mile to the prison camp to prevent the Germans from shooting him as a straggler. They both survived five months as prisoners of war.

Reports from Gerow of an all-out offensive failed to convince Hodges of the seriousness of the German attack, and he continued his assault on the Roer dams; moreover, First Army took five and a half hours to pass the news on to SHAEF. Eisenhower learned of the offensive at 4:00 P.M.

Earlier in the day Eisenhower had been promoted to General of the Army, the American equivalent to field marshal. Bradley was at Eisenhower's Versailles headquarters to celebrate his West Point classmate's promotion when SHAEF learned of the German attacks, and like Hodges, he pronounced it nothing more than a spoiling attack designed to take Allied pressure off the Roer and Saar fronts. Eisenhower, however, knew immediately that it was a counteroffensive, and he ordered both the Ninth and Third Armies to send an armored division to Hodges; he also alerted SHAEF's only reserve, the XVIII Airborne Corps, consisting of the 82nd and 101st Airborne Divisions, to stand by for deployment. Two days later the 82nd reached Werbomont and the 101st arrived in Bastogne.

On December 19, at a meeting at Bradley's rear headquarters in Verdun, Eisenhower greeted Bradley, Devers, Patton, and their key staff officers by saying, "The present situation is to be regarded as one of opportunity for us and not of disaster. There will be only cheerful faces at this conference table." The supreme commander extended Sixth Army Group's boundary to the north and west by nearly thirty miles (48km) to allow Gen. Patch's Seventh Army to take over the line formerly held by Patton. Eisenhower stopped all offensive action in order to hold the line of the Meuse. He asked Patton when he could move toward Bastogne, and Patton said he could attack on December 22 with three divisions. True to his word, Patton attacked in three days after pulling three divisions out of the line and turning them ninety degrees. It was Patton's singular moment of the war and would forever justify his reputation.

The Failure of Allied Intelligence

The Germans achieved surprise and a breakthrough, but despite all attempts to keep it a secret, both Ultra and the U.S.A.A.F.'s photo reconnaissance units located their preparatory buildup.

Von Rundstedt's role was critical because Allied intelligence officers believed that the old soldier would counterattack with his newly assembled panzer reserve, the Sixth Panzer Army, after the First U.S. Army crossed the Roer River. The First Army G-2, Col. Benjamin A. "Monk" Dickson, also noted that the enemy had the capability to launch "a concentrated counterattack with air, armor, infantry and secret weapons at a selected focal point at a time of his own choosing." Two days after Dickson's estimate of December 10, 12th Army Group issued one of the most unfortunate intelligence papers of the war. Directly rebutting Dickson, 12th Army Group's G-2 stated that "attrition is steadily sapping the strength of German forces on the Western Front and . . . the crust of defenses is thinner, more brittle and

more vulnerable than it appears on our G-2 maps or to the troops on the line."

Throughout the Ardennes, troops reported hearing tanks moving up to the front at night. German prisoners spoke of a Christmas offensive to retake Aachen for the Führer, and their morale underwent a dramatic improvement. A Luxembourg woman who crossed the front line reported seeing horse-drawn vehicles, engineering and bridging equipment, and soldiers with the distinctive SS uniforms. No Allied general credited the Germans with

Two regiments of the 106th Infantry Division—the 422nd and the 423rd—surrendered in the Schnee Eifel. The U.S. Army's official history calls the event the most serious defeat suffered by the U.S. Army during the campaign.

OPPOSITE, TOP: A German Tiger II, or "Royal" Tiger tank, carrying German paratroopers advances during the Battle of the Bulge. Each of these 75-ton (67.5t) monsters mounted an 88mm gun and had over 7 inches (185mm) of frontal armor. Fortunately for the Allies, few bridges in Europe could bear their weight and only 484 were produced.

BELOW: Two Germans advance past a burning American vehicle on December 18, near the village of Poteau, Belgium. After destroying elements of the already battered U.S. 14th Cavalry Group, the German 1st SS Panzer Division stopped to restage attacks for German newsreel photographers.

much offensive capability, however, and fewer still expected an offensive through the Ardennes, with its total lack of east-west roads. When SHAEF's G-2, Maj. Gen. Sir Kenneth Strong, warned Bradley about a German attack through the Ardennes, Bradley pointed out that the First Army had some 70,000 troops stationed there and that there were no suitable roads for an armored assault.

The SS in the Ardennes

Hitler designated Dietrich's Sixth Panzer Army (in January it became the Sixth SS Panzer Army) as the spearhead of the offensive so that the *Waffen*-SS (Armed-SS) would win a Nazi victory. The SS represented the shock troops of Nazi Germany and were known for brutality towards prisoners and civilians alike because the soldiers acted upon Nazi racial and political ideology.

Hitler saw that the SS panzer divisions got 500 new tanks and ninety Royal Tigers, 75-ton (67.5t) behemoths with 88mm guns and over 7 inches (185mm) of frontal armor. Lt. Col. Jochen Peiper led Kampfgruppe Peiper, made up of 4,000 men and 100 tanks and assault guns, along with eighty half-tracks, mostly from the 1st SS Panzer (*Liebstandarte Adolf Hitler*) and attached Volksgrenadiers; they shot hundreds of prisoners and Belgian civilians in the Ardennes in their failed race toward the Meuse. Before December 16 Peiper reminded his men of cleaning up Düren following an Allied "terror bombing" that left the remains of women and children scattered on streets and walls. They might not be able to stop a bomber, but they could kill Americans.

On December 17 at the Baugnez crossroads, two and a half miles (4km) south of Malmédy, Kampfgruppe

"The von Rundstedt Offensive"

Hitler returned von Rundstedt to command in the west after the Führer had decided to launch his offensive in the Ardennes. Von Rundstedt's caution and professionalism clearly misled Allied generals as to who was planning operations in the German army. After the war von Rundstedt said: "I strongly object . . . that this stupid operation in the Ardennes is sometimes called the 'von Rundstedt offensive.' That is a complete misnomer. I had nothing to do with it. It came down to me as an order complete to the last detail. . . . It was only up to me to obey. It was a nonsensical operation. . . . If we reached the Meuse we should have gotten down on our knees and thanked God—let alone tried to reach Antwerp."

Field Marshal Gerd von Rundstedt twice served as Hitler's dupe to mislead Allied intelligence: first in 1940 during the mythical invasion of England that von Rundstedt was supposedly going to command; second in 1944 when the old field marshal was seen as being too cautious and professional to attack through the Belgian Ardennes.

Peiper overcame Battery B, 285th Field Artillery Observation Battalion, as it turned onto the N23 toward St. Vith. Quickly destroying its vehicles, several SS herded the survivors into a field next to the road. Half-tracks opened fire with machine guns, as did passing tanks. SS troopers then walked among the wounded, shooting any man observed moving or groaning. Peiper's men killed eighty-six Allied soldiers at the crossroads. Later that day the SS would kill ninety Belgian civilians at Stavelot.

U.S. combat engineers held up Peiper for twelve hours at Stavelot on December 17 by blowing up the bridges at Trois-Ponts ("Three-Bridges") over the Amblève River and the Salm River, thereby forcing him to drive farther westward. At that time Maj. Gen. Elwood "Pete" Quesada, commander of the IX Tactical Air Command in support of the First Army, got two pilots to volunteer to fly the Amblève River valley.

Flying at less than 100 feet (30m), Quesada's pilots marked Kampfgruppe Peiper's route and location. Two strikes by P-47 Thunderbolts caught the German column

The German MG42 machine gun fired 1,200 rounds per minute, much more rapidly than Anglo-American counterparts, and used massive amounts of ammunition. This German carries a bandolier over his shoulder while the man behind him carries an ammunition box. Most Germans wore scarves under their helmets to retain some heat.

as it was crossing the bridge over the Amblève at Cheneux, destroying a Panther tank on the narrow road out of town. This delay gave engineers time to wire the next bridge on Peiper's westward movement for destruction, the timber trestle bridge over the Lienne Creek at Neufmoulin. Daylight was vanishing when Peiper's lead tank, a Royal Tiger, fired on the trestle bridge. Cpl. Fred Chapin ducked to avoid the explosion of the 88mm round and twisted the detonator, setting off 2,500

pounds (1135 kg) of TNT. Peiper saw his hopes of reaching the Meuse go up in smoke.

Accompanying Peiper was a task force of Lt. Col. Otto Skorzeny's Panzer Brigade 150, which was organized to operate behind American lines with English-speaking troops. The entire "Trojan-horse operation" depended upon U.S. vehicles and uniforms. Skorzeny had 150 soldiers out of 2,000 who could speak passable English, so he put his very best English

By the time American troops retook St. Vith on January 23, 1945, soldiers of the 7th Armored Division had received proper winter camouflage.

Two army group commanders
and two army commanders
meet along the Franco-German
border on an improved landing
strip, from left to right:
Lt. Gen. Jacob L. Devers
(6th Army Group),
Lt. Gen. George S. Patton, Jr.
(Third Army),
Lt. Gen. Alexander Patch
(Seventh Army), and
Lt. Gen. Omar Bradley
(12th Army Group).

speakers in forty teams of jeeps, of which all but eight returned to German lines.

These few men created havoc out of all proportion to their numbers. The German parachute drop on the night of December 17 caused mass confusion on the northern shoulder of the Bulge. The German commander of the paratroops, Col. Friedrich von der Heydte, von Stauffenberg's cousin, jumped into a 24 mph (38km) wind over the Haute-Fagnes-Eifel area, ten miles (16km) north of Malmédy; his mission was to hold the roads open for Dietrich's panzers that never got to Malmédy.

Ten of the 105 German aircraft dropped their paratroopers over the Haute-Fagnes between Spa and Monschau. Three days later von der Heydte surrendered with pneumonia and trench foot. On December 19 one of Skorzeny's men told his American captors that their mission was to kill Eisenhower, which led Eisenhower to live from that point under virtual house arrest.

Montgomery in Command

On December 20 at 10:30 A.M. Eisenhower put Montgomery in command of the northern half of the Bulge, which Eisenhower defined by a line running from Givet, France, through Houffalize, Belgium, to Prüm, Germany; this simplified control of the two flanks of the German penetration in the Ardennes.

Montgomery was now in tactical command of two American armies, Lt. Gen. William H. Simpson's Ninth Army and Hodges's First, while Bradley retained operational control of Patton's Third Army. Always against Eisenhower's and Bradley's twin thrusts, he came to First Army Headquarters with the largest Union Jack that would fit on the front of the car and eight motorcycle outriders—as one of his aides-de-camp put it, "like Christ come to cleanse the temple."

Montgomery asked for Collins to lead a corps for counterattack purposes and began creating a reserve with units from the Ninth Army, such as the 2nd Armored Division under Maj. Gen. Ernest Harmon, as well as the 84th Infantry Division under Brig. Gen. Alexander R. Bolling. On December 19 Montgomery had ordered General Horrocks's 30 Corps to backstop the Meuse River. Montgomery asked the commander of the 7th Armored Division outside St. Vith if he favored withdrawal to a more secure line and Maj. Gen. Robert W. Hasbrouck said that if he did not get out that night there would be no more 7th Armored Division. Therefore, Montgomery told Hodges to get them out to more secure positions. St. Vith had been von Manteuffel's objective on the first day of the offensive, but Hasbrouck and his Combat Command B Commander, Brig. Gen. Bruce Clarke, along with troops from the shattered 106th and 28th Divisions, had delayed Fifth Panzer Army in front of St. Vith for six days, ruining the German timetable.

When Eisenhower went to see Montgomery in Belgium on December 28, the Englishman scolded his superior, telling him that the German counteroffensive was the result of his twin failures: the broad-front strategy and the ground forces command. The next day the field marshal wrote a letter referring to Allied ground operations as "one very definite failure." Montgomery

A Malmédy Survivor

Pvt. Ted Paluch of Philadelphia was a member of Battery B, 285th Field Artillery Observation Battalion. German tanks overtook his American column, spraying it with machine-gun fire. Paluch jumped into a ditch and stayed there until a King Tiger lowered its 88mm gun in his direction. "They marched us up to the intersection, and they searched us," he later reported. "They took my cigarettes, watch. I had an extra pair of socks in my pocket; they took that."

Right after the SS troops left, the Germans opened fire with machine guns from half-tracks and tanks. Paluch said, "They were on the move, and they didn't have that many men. I guess they couldn't leave some men to guard us." Shot in the hand, Paluch played dead, while Germans walked among the moaning soldiers and killed them at close range. Paluch got up, ran for a hedge line, and again played dead until dark when he finally made it back to American lines.

even wrote the order for the Supreme Allied Commander to return him to operational control of the ground forces: "From now onwards full operational direction, control and co-ordination of these operations is vested in the C.-in-C. 21 Army Group, subject to such instructions as may be issued by the Supreme Commander from time to time."

Finally, Montgomery had found the limit of Eisenhower's patience, and Eisenhower and Bedell Smith drafted a letter for the Combined Chiefs of Staff telling them to choose between Eisenhower and Montgomery—one of them would have to go. Luckily for Montgomery, his Chief of Staff, Freddie de Guingand, got wind of the SHAEF ultimatum and went to talk to Eisenhower. De Guingand then flew to see his superior and informed him that Eisenhower was going to let the Combined Chiefs pick who should go—and that it would not be Eisenhower.

Montgomery remained unshaken until de Guingand added that Eisenhower and Smith would ask for

Field Marshal Sir Harold Alexander as Monty's replacement. At that point Montgomery allowed his Chief of Staff to draft a letter of apology that proved sufficient for the supreme commander to tear up his ultimatum to the Combined Chiefs. However, controversy continued to swirl around Montgomery.

The 101st Airborne at Bastogne

Brig. Gen. Anthony McAuliffe, the artillery commander of the 101st Airborne, commanded the division in Bastogne because Gen. Taylor, the commanding general, was in Washington, D.C., lobbying Congress for larger airborne divisions. By December 21 the Germans had surrounded Bastogne, and the next day several German officers approached bearing a white flag. Taken to McAuliffe, they told him that unless he surrendered they would pulverize Bastogne with artillery. McAuliffe laughed. As an artillery officer he knew that he was

Bastogne was a market town on a plateau where eight roads converged from surrounding villages. Because of its strategic value and relative open terrain, large armored units came together on the plateau. Note that the Sherman tank has backed down the slope to lower the amount of its profile visible from the approaching ridge line. Two soldiers man a .30 caliber machine gun to protect the tank from German infantry.

A German *Wirbelwind* (Whirlwind) antiaircraft self-propelled gun with four 20mm cannon stands as mute testimony to ferocious battle in the Bulge. Because of overwhelming Allied aerial supremacy German armored columns had to have their own antiaircraft vehicles. The Whirlwind was cobbled onto a Mark-IV chassis.

the 101st was able to cope with the best part of four German armored divisions.

At 4:50 P.M. on December 26 a tank battalion of the 4th Armored Division led by Lt. Col. Creighton W. Abrams, a future Chief of Staff of the United States Army, entered Bastogne. Trucks and ambulances followed along with Gen. Taylor, who had flown back from the United States; Taylor would lead the 101st in even worse fighting in the days to come as the Germans renewed their effort to take Bastogne, but this time Bastogne would not be cut off from American lines. Bastogne became the symbolic American victory of the German counteroffensive, proving that the Germans could not capitalize on their initial success.

Operation Nordwind

On January 7, 1945, the German Army Group G under Gen. Johannes Blaskowitz counterattacked to take advantage of Eisenhower's broad-front strategy and the American army's 90-Division Gamble.

When Devers's Sixth Army Group assumed the responsibility for Patton's frontage on December 19, the frontage of Gen. Patch's Seventh Army increased from 75 to 125 miles (120 to 200km), from Saarbrücken east to Lauterbourg and then south along the Rhine. Under Eisenhower's orders all offensive operations ceased in order to hold the line of the Meuse in Belgium. As a result, Eisenhower wanted Devers to pull back to the eastern slopes of the Vosges Mountains to shorten his lines, but that meant giving up Strasbourg.

Gen. Charles de Gaulle admitted that Strasbourg had no military value, but for France, losing it would be a national disaster. Condemning Strasbourg to another round of German occupation would be ruinous to its residents and to de Gaulle's reputation. Therefore, he instructed Gen. de Lattre to take preliminary steps to withdraw the 3rd Algerian Division out of the Vosges in preparation to defend Strasbourg.

Hitler saw Patch's front as a prop to his failing Ardennes offensive, and OKW came up with Operation Nordwind. The German attack in the Low Vosges directly threatened Strasbourg, and to prevent a diplomatic

inflicting severe punishment on the Germans, and as a paratrooper he had trained to fight completely surrounded.

On December 23 the weather cleared from England to Belgium, and the bombers, fighter-bombers, and fighters inflicted hideous punishment on the Germans. One of the pilots later told McAuliffe that Bastogne was "better hunting than the Falaise pocket." Support was so good that within twenty minutes of reporting tanks, P-47s would appear and kill them. It was such a tremendous relief after having been so short of ammunition earlier in the battle that McAuliffe had told one commander that if he saw "400 Germans in a 100-yard [91m] area, and they [had] their heads up, you [could] fire artillery at them—but not more than two rounds."

Two hundred forty C-47s dropped 140 tons (126t) of supplies, mainly artillery ammunition, and on December 24 another 100 tons (90t) arrived. Thanks to the firepower of attached units, two armored combat commands from the 4th and 10th Armored Divisions, as well as two field artillery and a tank destroyer battalion,

The Cost of the German Winter Offensives

The Germans shot their bolt in the Ardennes. After the failure of the Ardennes offensive in the west, von Manteuffel said that Hitler fought a "private's war," meaning that he only reacted to the Allies' maneuvers; he did not plan.

The Germans lost 67,000 men killed and wounded in the Ardennes and 23,000 in Alsace, while the Americans lost about 90,000 during Hitler's last offensives. For the Germans it meant the complete loss of their strategic reserve, in both men and tanks, west of the Rhine River; they could never make up those incredible losses.

The American army was still growing and was able to replace its losses in men and equipment. Despite the 90-Division Gamble and the replacement shortage, new divisions would continue to arrive from the United States until the final weeks of the war. The Germans had no strategic reserves left to meet the Russian winter offensive in mid-January and had to redeploy troops from southern France to the eastern front, which was growing closer and closer to Berlin.

disaster, Eisenhower reversed himself and ordered Devers to hold Strasbourg at all costs. While Strasbourg distracted the Franco-Americans, the Germans crossed the Rhine and made a bridgehead for themselves between Drusenheim and Gambsheim, forcing the Americans to withdraw behind the Moder River. Farther south the Germans created a large salient known as the Colmar pocket that took until February to reduce.

LEFT: Pfcs. Joseph Latrell (left) of Whitehall, New Jersey, and Harry Fafer (right) of Passaic, New Jersey, guard SS Storm Troopers. After Malmédy, few SS troopers were taken alive. Notice the attention given by the German in the second row to Fafer's rifle pointed in his direction. BELOW: Six miles (9.6km) from Bastogne, tanks of the Third Army mass prior to their final push into the area to relieve the surrounded Americans. The smoke in the left rear portion of the photograph is from recent American artillery fire on German positions.

Chapter 5

The Defeat of Germany

ONE MONTH AFTER THE BATTLE OF THE BULGE HAD BEGUN, THE FIRST AND Third U.S. Armies rejoined at the Belgian roadnet town of Houffalize. Omar Bradley remembered it "as sleepy village on the side of a hill, ten miles north of Bastogne on the macadam road to Liège." To prevent Germans from gaining its east-west roadnet, U.S. strategic bombers turned its buildings into rubble and its roads into craters, which Third Army bulldozers filled with the rubble. "Simple, poor, and unpretentious, the village had offended no one," Bradley said. "Yet it was destroyed because it sat astride an undistinguished road junction."

The Red Army's massive winter offensive began on January 12 and commanded Hitler's return to Berlin. By February 7 three Russian army fronts (each equivalent to an Anglo-American army group) had advanced 280 miles (448km) from the Vistula, across Poland, and into East Prussia. Averaging fourteen miles (22km) a day, the Red Army seized the industrial region of Upper Silesia, which forced the Germans to depend almost exclusively on the Ruhr for all their war matériel. Coming to a halt at Küstrin on the Oder River, Marshal Georgi Zhukov's First Belorussian Front was only fifty miles (80km) from the German capital. Hitler's newly promoted Chief of the Army General Staff Heinz Guderian warned Hitler before the Russian attack that the eastern front was "a house of cards" that would collapse if penetrated at a single point, but Hitler had sacrificed Germany's armored reserves in his Ardennes counteroffensive and had no answers for the eastern front, much less any armies to spare.

LEFT: The pride of Germany when first built in the 1930s, the autobahn was serving the mobility of the U.S. army by March 1945. Columns of two-and-a-half-ton (2.3t) trucks ("deuce and a halfs") kept pace with Sherman tanks, now up gunned (equipped with a better caliber of gun) to face German tanks. Meanwhile thousands of German prisoners marched to prisoner of war camps in the rear.

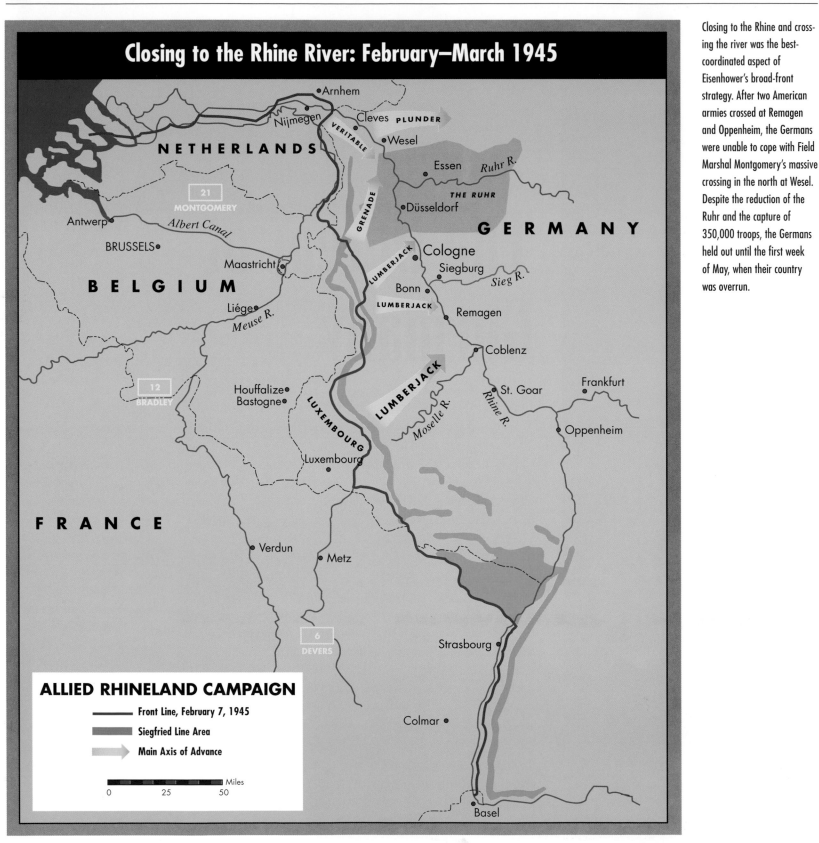

Closing to the Rhine River: February–March 1945

NETHERLANDS

Arnhem

Nijmegen

Cleves

PLUNDER

VERITABLE

Wesel

Essen

Ruhr R.

THE RUHR

GRENADE

Düsseldorf

GERMANY

Antwerp

Albert Canal

21
MONTGOMERY

BRUSSELS

Maastricht

Cologne

Siegburg

LUMBERJACK

Bonn

Sieg R.

BELGIUM

Liége

Meuse R.

LUMBERJACK

Remagen

Coblenz

Houffalize

Bastogne

12
BRADLEY

LUXEMBOURG

LUMBERJACK

Moselle R.

St. Goar

Frankfurt

Rhine R.

Luxembourg

Oppenheim

FRANCE

Verdun

Metz

6
DEVERS

Strasbourg

Colmar

ALLIED RHINELAND CAMPAIGN

— Front Line, February 7, 1945

■ Siegfried Line Area

➤ Main Axis of Advance

Miles

0   25   50

Basel

Closing to the Rhine and crossing the river was the best-coordinated aspect of Eisenhower's broad-front strategy. After two American armies crossed at Remagen and Oppenheim, the Germans were unable to cope with Field Marshal Montgomery's massive crossing in the north at Wesel. Despite the reduction of the Ruhr and the capture of 350,000 troops, the Germans held out until the first week of May, when their country was overrun.

On January 16, Hitler left his western front head-quarters and took up residence in his underground bunker below the garden of the Reich Chancellery in Berlin. In extending the Chancellery's air-raid shelter in 1944, Albert Speer, Hitler's architect, had designed eighteen rooms on two floors some fifty feet (15m) underground and protected by a concrete roof sixteen feet (5m) thick, which he covered with more than thirty feet (9m) of earth.

The *Führerbunker* had its own electrical, water, and power supplies, as well as bathing and cooking facilities. For the last 105 days of his life, Hitler lived in six cramped rooms of this underground warren because the Allies had won the air war over the Reich and the Chancellery itself was unlivable. Going underground, Hitler initiated the final battle for Germany.

The Malta and Yalta Conferences

At the end of January 1945, the Combined Chiefs of Staff met on the Mediterranean island of Malta, prior to the February meeting of Roosevelt, Churchill, and Stalin at Yalta in the Crimea. The Malta conference was Churchill's idea, and the British Chiefs of Staff requested an explanation of Eisenhower's future plans. The British Chiefs brought two recommendations of their own: one, that the Combined Chiefs of Staff direct Eisenhower to make his main thrust in the north against the Ruhr; two, that Eisenhower name a ground forces commander. The British got their first point but not their second, and both sides harbored resentments.

At the Yalta Conference British diplomats were shocked by President Roosevelt's physical appearance;

ABOVE: General Heinz Guderian was the father of the German tanks corps. Author of *Achtung Panzer!* (*Attention Tanks!*) in 1935, he commanded armored corps in Poland, France, and Russia, where he was relieved in December 1941. Named Inspector General of Armored Troops in 1943, Guderian became Chief of the Army General Staff until relieved again in late March 1945. LEFT: Churchill, Roosevelt, and Stalin met for the last time at Yalta, in the Crimea, in mid-February 1945, to plan the postwar future of Europe. Churchill's physician, Lord Moran (Sir Charles Wilson), was shocked by the President's appearance and gave him "only a few months to live." Roosevelt was dead within two months of Yalta.

RIGHT: This soldier from the Ninth U.S. Army was killed by mortar fire on February 23, 1945, while crossing the Roer River during Operation Grenade. The men behind him on the footbridge are stretcher bearers who are about to retrieve a wounded man not in the photograph. BELOW: In February and March 1945 the rains thawed frozen overused roads in the low countries and the result was an impassable sea of mud. A British soldier attempts to free his jeep from mud near Arnhem.

he would die two months later. The United States sought and got Stalin's promise to enter the war against Japan within three months of the end of the European war; the atomic bomb was untested and an Allied invasion of Japan loomed.

Yalta also produced boundaries for the occupation zones of Germany, placing Berlin some 150 miles (240km) inside the Soviet zone. All three powers were to receive a piece of Berlin, but during the Yalta conference, SHAEF's armies were approaching the Roer and the Rhine Rivers, some 250 miles (400km) from the German capital, while the Russians were far closer, giving them a strong geographical advantage over the Anglo-Americans.

Closing to the Rhine

Eisenhower had eighty-five divisions for the final assault on the Reich—two thirds of them American. He allotted thirty-five to Montgomery's northern thrust designed to cross the Rhine just north of the Ruhr. Committing twenty divisions for the defense of the Rhine and twenty-five for Bradley's secondary assault on the Ruhr from the south as well as an advance on Frankfurt left the remainder to constitute SHAEF reserve.

Above all, Eisenhower wanted to close to the length of the Rhine in order to destroy the German army west of the river, which would speed the final German collapse and let him hold the Rhine with only twenty divisions while Montgomery's northern attack proceeded. Without closing to the Rhine, Eisenhower feared that he might have to keep forty-five divisions west of the river to finish clearing out the Siegfried Line. Eisenhower's three-step plan represented the culmination of his broad-front strategy.

Operations Veritable and Grenade

Montgomery gave the First Canadian Army the task of clearing the Reichswald, the German state forest at the northern terminus of the Siegfried Line, and to assist in the task he gave Crerar's army Horrocks's British 30 Corps; three quarters of the troops were British on loan from Dempsey's British Second Army while it planned the crossing of the Rhine.

Horrocks had to widen the frontage to create room for Lt. Gen. Guy Simonds's 2nd Canadian Corps. RAF Bomber Command leveled Cleves, home of Henry VIII's fourth wife, with 1,400 tons (1,260t) of bombs, including 12,000-pound (5,443kg) Blockbuster bombs. The RAF ignored Horrocks's request that it use only incendiary bombs on the approaches into Cleves, and the craters and rubble slowed Horrocks's advance.

Operation Veritable was to gain control of the west bank of the Rhine. Its artillery barrage was the greatest of the war in northwest Europe up to that time; more than 1,000 guns fired for three hours and then ceased firing, which tempted the German artillery to open fire. Using sound and flash location techniques, the Anglo-Canadian artillery then opened counter-battery fire for an additional two and a half hours. Half a million shells fell on the seven-mile (11km) front of the German 84th Infantry Division.

Twenty-first Army Group had planned Veritable to take place in January, but the Battle of the Bulge intervened. Steady rain from February 2 to February 10 thawed the ground and melted the winter snow, and the Roer, Rhine, and Maas Rivers rose accordingly. The ground between the Maas and the Rhine came to resemble an island. The result was a World War I–style battle fought in mud and water, and the traffic jams were mon-

umental; at one point a British column approaching Cleves, Germany, had its tail in Nijmegen, Holland. Horrocks said "it rained almost every day, added to which the Germans breached the banks of the Rhine, so instead of the lovely hard frozen 'going,' we were faced by oceans of mud and water and within ten minutes of the start every tank—in fact every vehicle—was bogged down and the water started to spread across our one road Nijmegen-Cleves."

Up against the Rhine the Canadian 3rd Infantry Division had to patrol and attack in boats, earning the nickname the "Water Rats" from their commander. Luckily the 21st Army Group enjoyed a large supply of dukws, buffalos (Landing Vehicle Tracks [LVTs]), weasels (amphibious jeeps), and kangaroos (armed

British tommies flush out a German sniper during the British Second Army's push east of the Maas River between Roermond and Geilenkirchen. One soldier rushes while the soldier at the lower left covers his comrade.

A British 40-ton (36t) Mark 4, Churchill tank is caught in the flood of February 15, 1945, near Kranenburg in the battle of the Reichswald about five miles (8km) from Cleves. The Germans had blown the levee on the Rhine River, flooding the entire Dutch-German frontier during Operation Veritable.

The German Schuh-mine

Germans still had millions of mines, and in the sodden Reichswald campaign the wooden German *Schuh-mine* (shoe-mine) proved devilishly effective because it could not be detected with the standard metal mine detector. About the size of a box of kitchen matches, a Schuh-mine contained a quarter-pound (114g) of TNT, which would easily blow off a man's foot.

The Ninth U.S. Army attempted to solve this problem by buying up every available pitchfork in liberated Holland and Belgium to turn over ground to find Schuh-mines. The quick method for dealing with the proliferation of Schuh-mines was to have a tank run over them and detonate them, and the infantry could follow safely in the tank's tracks.

personnel carriers) because without them there would have been no way to get food and ammunition to the frontline troops or to take out their wounded. Horrocks called it "the worst battle I ever experienced."

Eighty miles (128km) to the south, near Schmidt, Germany, on February 9 the Germans blew the sluice gates on the Roer River dams to flood the region. Downstream the Roer grew to more than 300 yards (275m) wide, ten times its normal width, delaying Operation Grenade, Ninth U.S. Army's crossing of the Roer and advance to the Rhine. While the Roer flowed too rapidly to cross safely, the Ninth Army was stuck behind it, and the Germans redeployed their forces to the north to face the First Canadian Army. The German First Parachute Army under Gen. Alfred Schlemm grew to nine divisions—three panzer, three infantry, and three paratroop divisions. Fuel shortages prevented their jump training, but 75 percent of Schlemm's paratroops were less than twenty-five years of age and grew up in the Hitler Youth. These "paratroops" still had faith in the Führer and the fatherland; they fought virtually to the last man.

On February 23 Ninth Army crossed the Roer at Jülich and Linnich. Once Simpson's eleven divisions broke out of their Roer River bridgeheads on February 25, however, the Germans found that their four depleted infantry divisions were unable to stop American armored columns that moved around the clock. Simpson's attack order stated: "Pursue the enemy relentlessly to the limit of every man's endurance."

Von Rundstedt tried to convince Hitler to withdraw behind the Rhine, but Hitler wanted the West Wall held "as long as humanly possible." As far as Hitler was concerned, withdrawal "would just mean moving the catastrophe from one place to another." Because Anglo-American bombing played havoc with German railways, and the Russians had captured Silesia (the last unbombed industrial region of the Reich), Hitler needed to prevent the Anglo-American artillery fire from interdicting German barge traffic. Ruhr coal traveled up the Rhine to the Lippe and Dortmund-Ems Canals and to the ports of northern Germany. However, one week after the First Canadian and Ninth U.S. Armies met at Geldern on March 3, Schlemm withdrew the last units of his army across the Rhine at Wesel.

Crossing the Rhine

The speed of the American armored advance, which continued through the nights of the first week of March, took the Germans unawares. As the 4th Armored Division pushed to the Rhine, a German corps commander received a rude surprise when he drove up to what appeared to be a German unit surrounding a tank. Looking down from his Sherman, Lt. Joe Liese asked, "Where do you think you're going?" "It looks like I'm going to the American rear," the German general quickly replied. On March 6 Patton wrote to his wife that his Third Army was "in a horse race with Courtney," Hodges's First Army. Patton added, "If he beats me, I shall be ashamed."

Also on March 6, Maj. Gen. John Milliken, commanding III Corps in the First U.S. Army, called Maj. Gen. John Leonard, commanding general of the

ABOVE: Combat Engineers quickly turned the Ludendorff railway bridge, also known as the Remagen bridge, into a road bridge for men and vehicles to assist in the buildup on the east bank of the Rhine. They closed the bridge on March 13, 1945, to begin structural repairs. LEFT: A GI looks down on the Ludendorff railway bridge from the heights of the hill called the Erpeler Ley on the east bank of the Rhine River. Capture of the Remagen bridge was another instance in which the First U.S. Army outpaced the more famous Third U.S. Army.

The Remagen Bridge

Hitler's policy of fighting west of the Rhine and blowing bridges at the last moment had worked for thirty of the thirty-one bridges over the river, but at Remagen the Germans had only 660 pounds (300kg) of commercial dynamite instead of the necessary 1,320 pounds (600kg) of military explosives.

Investigation showed that shell fire had severed the conduit leading to the downstream or northern truss explosives; therefore, only the upstream truss explosives went off. With all the bridge's weight born by the downstream truss, the bridge collapsed on March 17, killing twenty-eight and injuring one hundred American engineers who were repairing it. By this date, however, engineers had spanned the Rhine north and south of the Ludendorff bridge with pontoon and treadway bridges and the loss of the bridge was not felt.

The Ludendorff railroad bridge, spanning the Rhine River, collapsed on St. Patrick's Day, March 17, 1945.

9th Armored Division, and asked Leonard to look at his map. "Do you see that little black strip of bridge at Remagen? If you happen to get that, your name will go down in glory." The next day Leonard sent Brig. Gen. William Hoge's Combat Command B towards Remagen, and when Hoge's troops emerged from the woods north of Remagen around 1:00 P.M. on March 7, they were astounded—the 1,069-foot (326m) -long Ludendorff railway bridge still spanned the Rhine.

Turning to his task force commander, Lt. Col. Leonard Engeman, Hoge said, "Put some white phosphorous and smoke around the bridge so the Krauts can't see what we're doing, cover your advance with tanks and machine guns, then bring up your engineers and pull out those wires on the bridge because we're going to take that bridge." However, before Lt. Karl Timmerman's company could begin the assault, the Germans set off their explosive charges, and the bridge exploded and lifted off its piers. When the dust settled so had the bridge—back onto its foundations—and Timmerman's company crossed the bridge under intense and unrelenting fire.

A platoon of experimental T-26 Pershing tanks equipped with 90mm guns commanded by Lt. John Grimball fired white phosphorous rounds at the railroad tunnel and knocked out a machine gun in one of the bridge's towers on the east bank. Accompanying the infantry, Lt. Hugh Mott and two of his engineer sergeants pulled wires set by the Germans and threw charges into the river. Thirteen Americans won the Distinguished Service Cross for heroism that day.

Remagen was the "rivet in Hitler's neck," as First Army's G-2, Col. "Monk" Dickson, put it, and Hitler sought scapegoats for its capture. Throughout February he had sacrificed his forces west of the Rhine to protect barge traffic rather than withdraw behind it, and that decision was now a shambles. Hitler appointed a court-martial team with its own firing squad that sentenced five officers to death for their Remagen role; they joined the fairly large ranks of between 13,000 and 15,000 German soldiers executed by their own government during the war.

Morale among Wehrmacht units had declined since the Ardennes fiasco. On March 8 Hitler fired

LEFT, TOP: Near Remagen two MPs (Military Police), Pfc. Vernon Bradbury, of Abbeville, South Carolina (left), and Pfc. Robert L. Mims, of Laurens, South Carolina (right), guard the heavy pontoon bridge, which was named the Rozich, Blackburn, Tompkins Bridge in honor of the engineers who died constructing it. LEFT, BOTTOM: A German woman carrying her last worldly goods flees a fire set by a German saboteur in Seigburg, Germany, on April 13, 1945.

von Rundstedt as commander in chief in the west for the second time, replacing him with Field Marshal Albert Kesselring, Luftwaffe general and master of defensive warfare, from the Italian Theater. True to Hitler's decree, Kesselring refused Gen. Paul Hausser's plea to withdraw his Army Group G from the Saar-Palatinate, thereby sentencing Hausser's army group to destruction west of the Rhine weeks after the Americans had crossed the river farther to the north.

On March 23 Patton called Bradley to say that the night before, the 5th Division had crossed the Rhine at Oppenheim, ten miles (16km) south of Mainz. Days later the 89th Division of Third Army crossed near St. Goar and climbed the Lorelei, a huge rock that rose 430 feet (130m) above the Rhine, placing an American flag atop it.

Hitler's Nero Decree

Two days after the Remagen bridge collapsed, Hitler called for a scorched-earth policy. "All military, transport, communication, industrial, and supply facilities, as well as material assets within the Reich territory which

ABOVE: Field Marshal Albert Kesselring, von Rundstedt's replacement as Commander in Chief West, served on the German General staff in World War I and later helped found the German Air Force. Kesselring commanded air fleets in Poland and France before becoming a field marshal and commanding ground forces in Sicily and Italy, where he acquired a reputation as a genius in defensive warfare.

the enemy might . . . make use of for the continuation of his struggle . . . are to be destroyed."

Since his Rhineland strategy had failed, Hitler intended to destroy the Ruhr before the Anglo-Americans could capture it. When Speer protested that the so-called Nero decree would leave nothing with which to rebuild Germany after the war, Hitler told him, "If the war is lost then the nation is lost also."

Hitler's nihilism was not new. In September 1944, when American troops first invaded, Hitler dictated an editorial to the Nazi *Völkischer Beobachter* (*The Racial Observer*): "Not a German stalk of wheat is to feed the enemy, not a German mouth to give him information, not a German hand to offer him help. He is to find every footbridge destroyed, every road blocked—nothing but death, annihilation, and hatred will meet him."

For the rest of March, Speer traveled around Germany talking to generals and sympathetic local government officials to prevent implementation of the scorched-earth policy, which he said later would have returned Germany to the Middle Ages.

Operations Plunder and Varsity

Operation Plunder, 21st Army Group's assault crossing of the Rhine, was the biggest set-piece battle since the Normandy invasion, and its preparations were litanies of Allied largesse.

A smoke screen that reached two hundred feet (60m) high and fifty miles (80km) long hid the west bank of the Rhine for ten days. In the two weeks leading up to the crossing, Anglo-American bombers dropped 50,000 tons (45,000t) of bombs behind the bridgeheads and on the cities of the Ruhr. Artillery stocks amounted to 60,000 tons (54,000t). The crossings depended upon 37,000 Royal Engineers as well as 22,000 U.S. Army engineers building numerous pontoon and treadway bridges across the Rhine; Ninth U.S. Army engineers even built a semipermanent railway bridge. Both the Royal Navy and the U.S. Navy stood by with landing craft to ferry troops, tanks, artillery, and ammunition across the Rhine, which was 300 to 500 yards (275–460m) wide and contained by dikes sixteen feet (5m) high.

LEFT: Engineers of the 87th Infantry Division ferry a tank across the Moselle River on March 16, 1945, in support of Third Army's attack on Koblenz. Behind them, the grapes that produce Moselle wine ripen in the sun.

LEFT: Troops of Patton's Third Army push into Weinburg, Germany, on April 22, 1945, eighteen miles (29 km) from the Czechoslovakian border. Advancing units found that front lines scarcely existed owing to the scattered German resistance, severed German communications, and a near total lack of German gasoline supplies.

LEFT: Men of the Third Army's 89th Division crossed the Rhine at St. Goar and Oberwessel on March 24-25, 1945. These men are under fire and have hunkered down in their dukw in hopes of making it to the other side of the Rhine alive. This photograph captures the utter vulnerability of infantrymen under fire. RIGHT: Soldiers from the 6th Armored Division, Third Army, reached Sachsenhausen, a suburb of Frankfurt, on March 26, 1945, and captured a bridge across the Main River suitable for infantry. The Germans fought back with artillery, destroying the town and setting it on fire.

Capt. Steel Brownlie's new Comet tank of the British 11th Armored Division carries infantrymen toward Petershagen on the Weser River, thirty miles (48 km) west of Hanover, in early April 1945. With four-inches (102 mm) of frontal armor and its 17-pound (8 kg) gun (76.2 mm, 3-inch) the British finally had a tank to stand up to the German Panthers and Tigers.

At 10:00 P.M. on March 23 the 1st British Commandos began to cross the Rhine in amphibious vessels. Minutes later they were across. Overwhelming artillery fire left the Germans stunned. More than 5,000 guns fired up and down the river and as far east as Essen. In the morning Bomber Command again hit Wesel, after which just 3 percent of its structures were still standing. After the bombardment, a German general approached a British commando, who told him to surrender. "I am General Friedrich Deutsch and I will only surrender to an officer of equal rank," the general replied, holding his pistol. "Well, this will equalize you," the lance corporal said as he machine-gunned Deutsch. Brig. Gen. Derek Mills-Roberts, commander of the 1st Commando Brigade, was so furious that as punishment he ordered the man to bury the German.

Operation Varsity, the airborne drop, brought out General Eisenhower, Prime Minister Churchill, and Field Marshal Brooke on March 24. To avoid the

tragedy of Arnhem, the drops took place within range of 21st Army Group's guns, and all the troops came in on one wave. The British 6th Airborne Division landed at the exits of the northern bridgeheads and the U.S. 17th Airborne Division at the southern exits. The airborne divisions came in on 1,600 planes and 1,300 gliders that required two and a half hours to cross the Rhine. Two thousand fighters flew air cover. German antiaircraft shot down more than 100 gliders and planes, but 21,000 paratroops landed successfully. Watching the airborne spectacle, Churchill said to Eisenhower, "My dear General, the German is whipped. We've got him. He is all through."

Across the Rhine the Germans were unable to cope with the immensity of the assault and the mobility of the Allies. However, the Allies found that they had to oust German paratroopers in house-to-house fighting, and individual German paratroopers would often fix their bayonets and charge. By March 28 the 21st Army Group had twenty divisions and 1,000 tanks across the Rhine, and its bridgehead was thirty-five (56km) miles wide and twenty-five (40km) miles deep.

While touring the bridgehead, Maj. Gen. Thomas Rennie, commander of the 51st Highland Division, died when a mortar round hit his jeep; Rennie was the only British division commander killed in the campaign. The casualties in 21st Army Group for the Rhine crossing came to 6,800 killed and wounded, more than a thousand of which occurred in the two airborne divisions. The British Second Army lost 4,000, and the Ninth U.S. Army took 2,800 casualties. German losses in the Rhineland campaign, on both sides of the river, came to 60,000 killed and wounded and more than a quarter of a million prisoners.

The Reduction of the Ruhr

On April 1, 1945, Easter Sunday, the Ninth U.S. Army swung north of the Ruhr and met the First U.S. Army at Lippstadt, some seventy-five miles (120km) due east of Wesel on the Rhine, trapping a third of a million Germans. Inside the Ruhr pocket were the remnants of Army Group B, the headquarters of the German

The French Crossing

When the Big Three at Yalta assigned one another postwar occupation zones, they excluded the French, who by then had eleven divisions in the fighting, and Gen. de Gaulle wanted a French zone of occupation befitting a European power.

De Gaulle cabled Gen. de Lattre on March 28: "You must cross the Rhine, even if the Americans do not agree and even if you have to cross it in rowboats. It is a matter of the greatest national interest." De Lattre, in anticipation of de Gaulle's dictate, had talked to his army group commander, Gen. Devers, who allowed him to extend the French zone of operations northward. On March 31 de Lattre sent units across the Rhine at Speyer.

France's honor was assuaged by the men of the 3rd Algerian Infantry Division, who took all night to cross ten at a time in a single rubber boat. Before dawn the discovery of four more rubber boats greatly speeded the division's progress. Such crossings said more about the lack of German opposition than French preparation, but from the courage of its colonial troops France would eventually gain an occupation zone granted at the largesse of the Americans.

Fifteenth Army, two corps of the First Parachute Army, and the entire Fifth Panzer Army.

True to his instructions from Hitler, Field Marshal Model would not capitulate. One of his corps commanders, Gen. Friedrich Köchling, wrote, "The continuation of resistance in the Ruhr pocket was a crime. It was Model's duty to surrender . . . only the danger of reprisals against my family prevented me from taking this step myself." On April 15 Model simply disbanded his army group by discharging his troops. When Gen. Ridgway sent an emissary to Model in an attempt to get him to surrender, Model said, "A field marshal does not become a prisoner. Such a thing is not possible." The next day he drove into a forest near Düsseldorf and shot himself.

On April 18, resistance ended in the Ruhr. First and Ninth Armies had captured some 317,000 Germans and more than thirty generals. Veterans of the once proud Wehrmacht that had goose-stepped down the Champs Elysées now marched off to become prisoners in their own homeland.

The Race to the Elbe

After the Ninth U.S. Army made contact with Bradley in the Kassel-Paderborn area, Eisenhower had planned

The 11th Armored Division (Third Army) liberated Mauthausen concentration camp on May 5, 1945. The soldiers found a communal grave with 10,000 bodies in it. Of the 110,000 prisoners some 3,000 died following liberation when they ate rich foods, such as chocolate, that their bodies simply could not digest.

for it to revert to Bradley's command. Thereafter, Montgomery would provide flank protection to Bradley's army group, which would constitute the main thrust toward the Elbe. Eisenhower would cut Germany in half across its middle—east to west—on a line Erfurt-Leipzig-Dresden, with a secondary thrust aimed at Regensburg, Bavaria, and Linz, Austria.

Churchill and the British Chiefs complained mightily but soon recognized that at this stage of the war there was little Britain could do to change the supreme commander's decision. American power and prestige dominated the alliance in the final weeks of the war.

Yalta had established no manner for coordinating the ground effort in the closing days of the war as the western and eastern armies approached each other. There had already been one incident in Yugoslavia where American P-51s strafed a Soviet column, killing a corps commander and eleven others. Therefore, Eisenhower established a stop line at the Elbe and Mulde Rivers to prevent confusion and friendly-fire casualties.

As far as Berlin was concerned, Bradley estimated its capture would result in 100,000 casualties; moreover, Berlin lay 150 miles (240km) within the Soviet postwar zone of occupation. Bradley was Eisenhower's chief operational adviser by this time, and he did not want the Anglo-Americans to take 100,000 casualties for a prestige objective that they soon would split with the Russians. The Yalta accords guaranteed Russian, British, and American occupation zones of Berlin, and no Western statesman or soldier suggested that the Anglo-Americans go back on their word to the Soviets. As it turned out, the Russians took more than 300,000 casualties in their assault on Berlin.

On April 4 Bradley's 12th Army Group consisted of the First, Third, Ninth, and the newly constituted Fifteenth Army, under Gen. Gerow, assigned to the Rhine and the Ruhr mop-up. Bradley's was the largest ground force ever commanded by an American general. When the 2nd Armored Division of the Ninth Army became the first American unit to reach the Elbe River at Schönebeck on April 11, it had covered 200 miles (320km) in just fourteen days.

The next day the division crossed the Elbe and discovered the attention that being so close to Berlin

brought. The Luftwaffe attacked its bridgehead more than 400 times during its first week on the Elbe. On April 14 the German counterattacks against Combat Command B of the 2nd Armored overran the bridgehead.

Once the Allies crossed the Rhine they began liberating German concentration camps. The British arrived at Bergen-Belsen three weeks after a young Dutch girl named Anne Frank died there. In the Harz Mountains, the 3rd Armored Division liberated "Dora," part of the Nordhausen complex, where throughout the war 60,000 slave laborers had made V-1s and V-2s in underground tunnels; two thirds of the work force had perished. The SS calculated that on 900 calories a day most people would die within three months.

Eisenhower visited the Ohrdruf Nord concentration camp with Patton on April 13 and described what he saw to Marshall.

In one room, where there were piled up twenty or thirty naked men, killed by starvation, George

The Death of Maj. Gen. Maurice Rose

Son of a rabbi, Maj. Gen. Maurice Rose served in the American Expeditionary Force in World War I. A veteran tanker with service in North Africa, Sicily, and Normandy, his 3rd Armored Division set a record by moving 109 miles (174km) in one day following the breakout from the Remagen bridgehead.

East of the Ruhr, approaching the SS tank training school at Paderborn on March 30, four German Tiger tanks cut off Rose's column. After running Rose's jeep into a tree the nervous tank commander motioned for Rose and his subordinates to drop their pistol belts. Most of the Americans wore shoulder holsters that they dropped without lowering their arms, but Rose wore a pistol belt. When Rose lowered his arms to release the belt, the German tanker misconstrued Rose's actions and shot him dead. Rose had once told his superior, Maj. Gen. J. Lawton Collins, that he only knew how to lead his division from the front, and that was where he died.

OPPOSITE: Troops of the 63rd Infantry Division enter Waldenburg on April 16, 1945, just north of Schwabisch Hall. "Their towns were as bad as their factories," the original wartime caption read. "What can you do if they kept fighting when they knew doggone well they were licked?"

Although contact between American and Russian forces took place at Torgau on the Elbe River on April 25, 1945, the public was not informed until two days later. Once again, the First U.S. Army had upstaged its competition.

Patton would not even enter. He said he would get sick if he did so. I made the visit deliberately, in order to be in position to give firsthand evidence of these things if ever, in the future, there develops a tendency to charge these allegations merely to "propaganda."

It was a grim reminder that Hitler's Germany was a locus of race war, slave labor, and murder. Throughout Germany during the spring of 1945 Anglo-American commanders forced Germans who lived near these charnel pits to witness the millions of dead bodies. In many instances Allied soldiers conscripted German labor to bury them.

All that was left was to meet up with the Russians, which the 69th Division of the First U.S. Army did on April 25. Lt. Albert L. Kotzebue was leading a jeep patrol into Leckwitz two miles (3km) west of the Elbe when his men spotted a cavalryman—he was a Russian soldier. Quite apprehensive, the Russian rode off, and so did Kotzebue's men, straight toward the Elbe, where they quickly commandeered a boat, rowed across to Strehla, and contacted the 175th Rifle Regiment, 58th Guards Division.

Another 69th Division patrol under Lt. William D. Robertson saw strange helmeted soldiers on the wreckage of the Torgau highway bridge. Climbing onto the wreckage, Robertson met a Russian in the middle of the Elbe River. Unable to speak each other's language, they communicated by the universal language of soldiers: they pounded on each other's backs.

Hitler's Götterdämerung

To comfort Hitler in early April, Dr. Joseph Goebbels, the German propaganda minister, read to him from Thomas Carlyle's *History of Frederick the Great*. Goebbels read Carlyle's description of the winter of 1761–62 during the Seven Years' War when Frederick had planned to commit suicide until news arrived that the Russian empress had died and her pro-Prussian son wanted peace.

On April 12 Goebbels called Hitler to say, "My Führer, I congratulate you! Roosevelt is dead. It is written in the stars that the second half of April will be the turning point for us. This is Friday 13 April. It is the turning point." There would be no turning point. Instead, Hitler's mistress, Eva Braun, arrived on April 15 to die with Hitler and in time for his last birthday on April 20; he was fifty-six.

The Red Army launched its three-prong offensive against Berlin on April 16, and by April 22, it had surrounded the city. That same day *Reichsmarschall* Hermann Göring, Hitler's legally designated successor, cabled to request power to surrender for the best interests of Germany, infuriating Hitler. When Eva Braun's brother-in-law, SS Lt. Gen. Hermann Fegelein, deserted his post in the Führerbunker, Hitler had him shot.

As of April 26, the Russians were less than a mile (1.6km) from the bunker, and they began shelling the Chancellery. Two days later the Propaganda Ministry passed on a BBC broadcast citing Reuter's in Stockholm that *Reichsführer* Heinrich Himmler, in secret negotiations with Count Folke Bernadotte of the Swedish Red Cross, had offered to surrender to the West.

Himmler's treachery confirmed Hitler's decision to kill himself. Fourteen years earlier, and two years before

he came to power, Hitler had described to Hermann Rauschning, the President of the Danzig Senate (a League of Nations mandate in the Polish corridor, formerly east Prussia), how he would wage war when he took over the government. Unlike World War I there would be no surrender. If he lost the war, then he would drag the world down with him, he promised, and he began to hum the motif of the grand conflagration of Wagner's *Götterdämerung*.

On the night of April 29 Hitler married Eva Braun and dictated his last will and testament, which named Adm. Karl Dönitz, head of the German Navy, his successor, and blamed the Jews for starting the war. At around 3:00 P.M. on April 30 Adolf and Eva Hitler together committed suicide. She bit a plastic cyanide pellet, and he shot himself at the same instant she bit into the cyanide. SS guards burned their bodies in a shallow grave in the Chancellery garden. At 9:40 P.M. on May 1 German radio played excerpts from Wagner's *Götterdämerung* followed by the slow movement from Bruckner's Seventh Symphony written for Wagner's death. An announcer then said that Hitler had fallen "fighting to the last breath against Bolshevism."

"One could smell Wobelein Concentration Camp before seeing it," wrote Maj. Gen. James Gavin, commanding officer of the 82nd Airborne Division, "and seeing it was more than any human being could stand." Gavin ordered the nearby townspeople of Ludwigslust through the facility and later had them bury the dead. In the final days of the war, the mayor of Ludwigslust refused to feed the inmates and one fourth of the 4,000 political prisoners starved to death; the mayor, his wife, and their daughter all committed suicide.

RIGHT: Sgt. Ernest Pappas of Modesto, California, and the 2nd Armored Division examines Hitler's bunker in October 1945. Pappas has claimed five coat hangers and a large ring of Chancellery keys formerly belonging to Hitler. Note the water on the floor, which accumulated as soon as the pumps and dehumidifying equipment were not running.

BELOW: In the last known picture of the two friends together, Gen. Eisenhower and Gen. Patton are seen attending an inter-army football game on October 15, 1945, one week after Eisenhower fired Patton from command of Third Army for comparing the Nazis to the Republicans and the Democrats. Patton would die from injuries sustained in an automobile accident before the year was out.

On May 1, 1945, American tanks moved into the walled city of Nuremberg, formerly the site of annual Nazi Party rallies. Coincidentally, Nuremberg had fallen on April 20, Hitler's birthday. Hitler had often told Germans to give him five years and they would not know their cities, a promise which turned out to be true, though not in quite the way he had intended.

Germany Surrenders

Unlike World War I, when the German generals abdicated their responsibility to the nation and refused to sign the armistice, this time the German Wehrmacht surrendered for the military and the state.

On April 29 the German army in Italy surrendered unconditionally, to take effect on May 2. Montgomery accepted on May 4 the surrender of all German forces in northern Germany, Denmark, Holland, and the Frisian Islands. The next day German representatives appeared at Eisenhower's headquarters in Reims to discuss surrender. In actuality Dönitz was stalling for time to allow more German troops to escape the advancing Russians in order to surrender instead to the Western Allies.

Eisenhower informed him that he would seal the front unless the Germans surrendered unconditionally.

On May 7, 1945, Gen. Hans Jodl, Chief of Operations Staff of OKW, signed the surrender at Eisenhower's headquarters, and the war in Europe was to end at 11:01 P.M. on May 8, which became V-E Day, the day of Victory in Europe. The Soviets refused to come to a French city in order to accept Germany's surrender when they had captured the German capital and insisted on a separate surrender ceremony in Berlin on May 9, where Marshal Zhukov presided and Field Marshal Keitel signed for Germany.

It was eleven months since the Anglo-Americans had landed at Normandy, and although they did not have the prestige of capturing Berlin, the Allies accomplished

ABOVE: Hitler appointed Adm. Karl Dönitz his successor after Göring and Himmler made surrender overtures. Dönitz was the father of the German submarine service, and in January 1943 Hitler appointed him to command of the German Navy. Remaining loyal to Hitler, Dönitz refused to surrender until large numbers of German soldiers had escaped to the west and the Anglo-Americans rather than endure capture by the Russians. RIGHT: Field Marshal Wilhelm Keitel, head of OKW (High Command of the German Armed Forces), signs the unconditional surrender of Germany on May 9, 1945, in Berlin at a Soviet ceremony. Keitel was found guilty of war crimes by the International Military Tribunal at Nuremberg and was executed by hanging.

The British held a victory parade in Berlin on July 22, 1945, and the tanks and armored cars seen here belong to the 7th Armored Division, the "Desert Rats," who were veterans of five years of fighting the Germans and Italians. In the background is the German victory column, while the British victory column proceeds.

what they had set out to do. Eisenhower had led the most successful military coalition in history across disputed waters and onto fortified beaches against the military machine that had held the European continent in sway for four years.

From Normandy to the Elbe the United States suffered more than 586,000 casualties, of which 135,600 died. The British suffered 142,000 casualties, of which 30,000 occurred in the six weeks' time it took to fight from the Rhine to the Elbe. The Germans' casualties from Normandy to the Elbe numbered some 837,000, of which about 100,000 were dead.

For most of the campaign across northwest Europe the Germans held the numerical advantage and had fought on the defensive armed with superior weapons. They continued to fight even after Hitler had killed himself, and they stopped fighting only when they had no other choice, when they were overrun.

Bibliography

Ambrose, Stephen E. *D-Day, June 6, 1944: The Climactic Battle of World War II.* (Simon and Schuster, 1994).

Ambrose, Stephen E. *Citizen Soldiers: The U.S. Army from the Normandy Beaches to the Bulge, to the Surrender of Germany, June 7, 1944 to May 7, 1945.* (Simon and Schuster, 1997).

Bartov, Omer. *Hitler's Army: Soldiers, Nazis, and War in the Third Reich.* (Oxford University Press, 1992).

Blumenson, Martin. *Breakout and Pursuit. (U.S. Army in World War II: The European Theater of Operations).* (Office of the Chief of Military History, U.S. Army, 1961).

Bradley, Omar. *A Soldier's Story.* (Henry Holt and Company, 1957).

Cole, Hugh, M. *The Ardennes: Battle of the Bulge. (U.S. Army in World War II: The European Theater of Operations).* (Office of the Chief of Military History, U.S. Army, 1965).

Dear, I.C.B. and M.R.D. Foot, et al. *The Oxford Companion to World War II.* (Oxford University Press, 1995).

D'Este, Carlo. *Decision in Normandy.* (E. P. Dutton, 1983).

—————. *Patton: A Genius for War.* (HarperCollins, 1995).

Eisenhower, Dwight D. *Crusade in Europe.* (Doubleday and Company, 1948).

Hamilton, Nigel. *Monty: Final Years of the Field Marshal, 1944-1976.* (McGraw-Hill, 1986).

Hinsley, F. H., et al. *British Intelligence in the Second World War: Its Influence on Strategy and Operations. Vol. III, Part II.* (Her Majesty's Stationery Office, 1988).

MacDonald, Charles B. *The Mighty Endeavor: The American War in Europe.* (William Morrow, 1986).

—————. *The Siegfried Line Campaign. (U.S. Army in World War II: The European Theater of Operations).* (Office of the Chief of Military History, U.S. Army, 1963).

Montgomery, Bernard Law. *The Memoirs of Field-Marshal the Viscount Montgomery of Alamein, K. G.* (Collins, 1958).

Murray, G. E. Patrick. *Eisenhower Versus Montgomery: The Continuing Debate.* (Praeger, 1996).

Neillands, Robin. *The Conquest of the Reich: D-Day to VE-Day: A Soldier's History.* (New York University Press, 1995).

Speer, Albert. *Inside the Third Reich.* (Macmillan, 1970).

Thompson, Julian. *The Imperial War Museum Book of Victory in Europe.* (Sidgwick and Jackson, 1994).

Warlimont, Walter. *Inside Hitler's Headquarters, 1939-45.* (Weidenfeld and Nicolson, 1964).

Weigley, Russell F. *Eisenhower's Lieutenants: The Campaigns of France and Germany, 1944-1945.* (Indiana University Press, 1981).

Wilmot, Chester. *The Struggle for Europe.* (Collins, 1952).

Photo Credits

Index

A

Aachen, assault on, *71*
Abrams, Creighton W., 98
Abwehr. See German intelligence
Achtung Panzer! (Guderian), *103*
African-American soldiers, 24
Afrika Korps, 16
Airborne units. *See also* Rangers
    (U.S.); *specific units*
Allied, 21–22
    German, *73*
    U.S., equipment of, 21, *21*
Air power, Allied. *See also* Bombing
    campaigns, Allied and Battle of
    the Bulge, 83
Air war in Europe, 8, *46*, 50,
Albert Canal, 63
    defense of, 73, *73*
    German flight to, 65
Alexander, Harold, 97
Allied Expeditionary Force, comman
    ders of, 13–16
Allied forces
    airborne units of, 21–22
    Broad Front strategy of, *62*, 69, 85,
        105
    casualties, 68–69, 85
        Autumn 1944, 87–88
        in capture of Berlin, 117
        D-day to close of war, 123
        Operation Varsity, 114
    contributions of, 9
    "Germany first" policy of, 8, 11
    interception of German cipher by,
        18, 50, 56, 73, 91
    naval power of, *39*
    shortages of ammunition, 98
    supply problems during pursuit to
        West Wall, 65
Allied intelligence. *See also* G-2
    deception plans of, 18–19
    failure of, prior to Battle of the
        Bulge, 91–92
Allied invasion of Brittany (D-day),
    12–35, *17, 38*
    British alternatives to, 11
    casualties of, 52
    German strategy against, 20
    plan for, 15, 16–17 size of, 13
    U.S. preferences for, 11 war prior
        to, 10–11
Allied invasion of Germany, 100–123
    stop line for, 117
    troop strength for, 104
Alsace, casualties in, 99
America/American. *See* United States
Ammunition, Allied shortages of, 98
Amphibious vehicles. *See also*
    Landing Craft
    British, *9*
    dukws, 26, *27*, 105, *112*
Antiaircraft guns, German

20mm, self-propelled, *98*
    88mm, *25, 47, 47*, 76, *92*
Antwerp, port at, 73
Arc de Triomphe, *58,* 59
Ardennes
    Allied defense of, 82, 85, *90*
    casualties in, 99
    German counteroffensive in,
        83–85, *82, 88–91, 93. See also*
        Battle of the Bulge
    cost of, to Germans, 99
    SS in, 92–96
Army Group B (German), 73, 75
    capture of, 114
Army Group G (German), 98, 109
Army Group H (German), *73*
Army Nurse Corps (Allied), *42*
Arnheim, assault on, 76
Arnheim Annie, 79
Arnold, Henry "Hap," *44*
Artillery, German, *23*
    antitank weapons, 72–73
    88mm guns, *25,* 76
    Krupp 88mm antiaircraft gun, *47, 47*
    horse-drawn, *83*
Artillery barrage, largest, *103*
Artillerymen, *49*
Assassination attempt against Hitler,
    52
    recovery from, 70
Atlantic, submarine warfare in, 8, 11
Atlantic Wall, 13, *16–17*, 20, 344
    defenses behind, 39–40
Attrition, war of (Nov. 1944), 85
Autobahn, *100*
Avranches
    assault on, 56
    German counterattack on, *38,*
        56–57, 65

B

Bastogne, 97–98, *97, 99*
Battle of Britain, 10–11
Battle of the Bulge, 81–99
    German plans for, 83–84
Battle of the Hedgerows, 39–40, *40,*
    41
    casualties in, 40
Bayerlein, Fritz, 50, 56
Bazookas, *43, 44*
Beachheads, linking of, after D-Day,
    37
Beach obstacles, on D-Day, *28, 34.*
    See also Mines
HMS *Belfast,* 30
Belgium, liberation of, 64, *64*
Bergen-Belsen Concentration Camp,
    liberation of, 117
Berlin British victory parade in, *123*
    casualties in capture of, 117
    Russian assault on, 119
Betts, T. J., 72
Blamey, Pat, 30
Blaskowitz, Johannes, 98
Blitzkrieg, 10. *See also* Mobile
    warfare

Blockbuster bombs, 105
Bocage, 39
Bolling, Alexander R., 96
Bombing campaigns, Allied, 105, 106
    in Ardennes, 93–95
    at Bastogne, 98
    at Cleves, 105
    during crossing of Rhine, 114
    before D-Day, 13, 64, *64*
    at Düren, 92
    at Falaise-Argentan pocket, 58–59
    impact on Germany, 106
    for Operation Cobra, 55–56
    as pre-invasion deception, 18
    prior to operation plunder, 111
Bombing campaigns, Japanese, 11
Boulogne, liberation of, 73
Bouncing Betty mines, 88
Bradbury, Vernon, *109*
Bradley, Omar, *44, 90*
    and Ardennes, 90, *90*
    and assault on Brest, 63
    and Battle of the Bulge, 101
    and capture of Berlin, 117
    and Falaise-Argentan pocket, 58
    and Operation Cobra, 55, 56, *56, 58*
    reaction to Broad Front strategy,
        69–70
    and supply problems, 63, 65
    and thrust to Elbe, 96, 115–117
Brandenberger, Erich, 85
Braun, Eva, 119
Brereton, Lewis, 74–75
Brest, assault on, 63, *63,* 64, *64, 66*
Britain
    casualties, D-day to close of war,
        123
    command of U.S. forces by, 69
    interception of German codes by, 18
    resistance to early Allied invasion,
        11, 15
British equipment
    amphibious vehicles, *9,* 105
    Blockbuster bombs, 105
    gliders, 21, *40*
    landing craft tank (LCT), *9*
    Mark IV Churchill tank, *106*
    90mm guns, *77*
    Spitfire aircraft, 59
    tanks, 45
        Comet, *114*
        Firefly, 45
        trucks, during race for West Wall,
            65–67
    Typhoon aircraft, 34, 50, 59
British Navy, 111
Broad Front strategy, *62,* 69, 85, 105
Brooke, Alan, 14, *33,* 114
Browning, Frederick A. M. "Boy,"
    75, 78
Browning Automatic Rifle (BAR), *60*
Brownlie, Steel, *114*
Brussels, liberation of, 61
Bryant, C. F., 27
Buffalo amphibious vehicle, *9,* 105,

Bulgarians, surrender of, 72–73
Butcher, Harry, 72

C

C-47 aircraft (U.S.), 98
Caen, 37, 40, *54*
    assault on, 48–52, 55
Calais, liberation of, 73
Camouflage, winter, *95*
Carentan, *50*
    capture of, 48
Casablanca meeting, *11*
Casualties
    Allied, 52, 68–69, 85
        D-day to close of war, 123
        in Ardennes and Alsace, 99
        in Autumn 1944, 87–88
        in Battle of the Hedgerows, 40
        in capture of Berlin, 117
        due to friendly fire, 55–56, 117
    German, 52–55, 72
        Autumn 1944, 87–88
        D-day to close of war, 123
    on Omaha Beach, 23
    during Operation Varsity, 114
    on Utah Beach, 23
CCS. *See* Combined Chiefs of Staff
Censors, wartime, *21, 42, 87*
Champs Elysées, *36, 58, 59, 59,*
Chapin, Fred, 95
Cherbourg
    capture of, 48
    port at, *46,* 64
Chief of Staff Supreme Allied
    Commander (COSSAC), 16–17
Chiefs of Staff (COS), British, 11
Chill, Kurt, 73
Churchill, Sarah, *16*
Churchill, Winston, *33, 103*
    and command of Montgomery, 70,
        117
    compassion of, 18
    meetings with Roosevelt, 11, *11,*
        15, *16*
    notable sayings of, 11, 13, 18, 68
    and Operation Varsity, 114
    and Teheran Conference, 15, *16*
    and Yalta Conference, *103,* 103–104
Cipher codes, German, Allied inter
    ception of, 18, 50, 56, 73, 91
Clarke, Bruce, 96
Clifford, Alexander, 61
"Closing the ring" strategy, 11
Codes, German, Allied interception
    of, 18, 50, 56, 73, 91
Collins, J. Lawton "Lightning Joe,"
    23, 48, *48,* 56, 117,
Colmar Pocket, 99
Combat Command B, 96, 108, 117
Combined Chiefs of Staff (CCS), 11
Comet tanks (British), *114*
Commanders of Allied Expeditionary
    Force, 13–16
Communications Zone of European
    Theatre of Operations (COMZ),
    64, 67

Bulgarians, surrender of, 72–73
Butcher, Harry, 72

Concentration camps
    Bergen-Belsen, liberation of, 117
    Eisenhower at, 117–118
    German atrocities at, *115,* 117–118,
        119
    liberation of, *115,* 117,
    Mauthausen, liberation of, *115*
    Nordhausen, 117
    Ohrdruf Nord, 117–118
    Patton at, 117–118
    starvation at, 117–118
    witnesses of, 118
    Wobelein, *119*
Cook, Julian, 78
COS (Chiefs of Staff), British, 11
COSSAC. *See* Chief of Staff
    Supreme Allied Commander
Cota, Norman "Dutch," 27, *36*
Counteroffensives, German
    in Ardennes, 88–91, 93. *See also*
        Battle of the Bulge
    cost of, to Germans, 99
    at Avranches, 56–57, 65
    on D-Day, 20, 34, 37
    December, 1944, 81
    Eisenhower and, 90–91
    Patton and, 91
Crerar, H. D., 58, *72,* 105
Cruelty of German army, 10
    atrocities at concentration camps,
        115, 117–118, *119*
Crusade, Allied invasion as, 8
Culin, Furtis G., Jr., 45

D

Daily Mail, 61
Daily Mirror, 72
Deception
    by Allies, 18–19
    by Germans, 29, 83, 93, 95–96
de Gaulle, Charles, 59, 98
    and partitioning of Germany, 115
de Guingand, Francis, 69, 97
de Lattre de Tasigny, Jean, 68, 98, 115
Dempsey, Miles, 52, 55, *72*
Denmark, German invasion of, 10
Deutsch, Friedrich, 114
Devers, Jacob L., 69, *96,* 98–99, 115
Dickson, Benjamin A. "Monk," 91,
    108
Dieppe, Canadian assault on, 17, 31
Dietrich, Josef "Sepp," *85,* 85, 89,
Dollman, Friedrich, 53
Dönitz, Karl, 119, 122, *122*
Double Cross. *See* Twenty Committee
    (XX)
Dukws, 26, *27,* 105, *112*
Dunkirk
    battle of, 16
    siege of, 73

E

Eastern front
    as drain on German resources, 9
    German weakness on, 101

Eastern troops *(Osttruppen)*, 21, 31
XVIII Airborne Corps, 91
8th Airforce (U.S.), 55
Eighth army (British), 16
VIII Corps (U.S.), 56, 89
8th Infantry Regiment (U.S.), *75*
82nd Airborne (U.S.), *20,* 21–22, 77,
    83, 91, 119
82nd Division (U.S.), 37
84th Infantry Division (German), 105
84th Infantry Division (U.S.), 96
85th Attack Infantry Division
    (German), 73
87th Infantry Division (U.S.), *84, 110*
88mm antiaircraft gun (German), *25,*
    47, 47, 76, *92*
89th Division, 3rd Army (U.S.), 109,
    112
Eisenhower, Dwight D., *14, 21, 120*
  assassination attempt on, 96
  assumption of command by, 15–16,
    69–70
  background of, 14–15
  Broad Front strategy of, *62,* 69, 85,
    105
  campaigns in North Africa in
    Mediterranean, 15
  defense of Strasbourg, 98–99
  doubts about Allied invasion, 14
  and German concentration camps,
    117–118
  and German counteroffensive,
    90–91
  and German surrender, 122
  and Montgomery, power struggle
    with, 96–97
  and Operation Varsity, 114
  pre-invasion speech of, 8
  promotion of, 90
  strategy of, at Battle of the Bulge,
    96
Eisenhower, Mamie Doud, 16
El Alamein, battle of, 16
Elbe, race to, 115–119
11th Armored Division (British), 52,
    61, 114, 115
Ellery, John, 34
Elsenborn Ridge, *86*
Engeman, Leonard, 108
Engineers, 93, 108, *107, 109*
  and Operation Plunder, 111
England. *See* Britain
Enigma cipher machine, 18, *19*
Executions of German soldiers by
    German army, 198

F
Fafer, Harry, *99*
Falaise, bombing of, *57*
Falaise-Argentan gap, battle of, 70
Falaise-Argentan pocket, 56–59
Fegelein, Hermann, 119
Ferguson, Kenneth, 32
5th Division (U.S.), 109
Fifth Panzer Army (German), 85, *86,*
    90, 96,
  capture of, 115

Fifteenth Army (German), 65, 74, 77
  headquarters, capture of, 114–115
Fifteenth Army (U.S.), 117
50th Armored Division (British), 52
50th Division (British), 30
51st Armored Division (British), 52
51st Highland Division (British), 114
51st Infantry Division (British), 51,
    73
58th Guards Division, 118
59th Infantry Division (British), 69
59th Division (German), 77
Finland, surrender of, 72–73
Firefly tanks, 45
1st Airborne (British), 75, 78–79, *79*
I Airborne Corps, 75
First Allied Airborne Army, 74
First Army (Canadian), 58, 73, 105,
    106
First Army (French), 68, 69
First Army (U.S.), 55–56, 58, *71,* 81,
    85, 93, *107,* 114, 115, 117
  and American contact with Russian
    forces, 118, *118*
  at Battle of the Bulge, 91, 96
  firsts by, 69
First Belorussian Front, 101
1st Commando Brigade (British), 114
1st Infantry Division (U.S.), *12,* 23,
    24
First Parachute Army (German), 73,
    106
  in Operation Varsity, 115
1st SS Panzer Division (German), 51,
    92
V Corps, 88
502nd Parachute Infantry (U.S.), *43*
506th Parachute Infantry Division
    (U.S.), *76*
FLAK, origin of term, 47
Flooding, strategic, by Germans, 106
Les Forges, *41*
Foucarville, *43*
4th Armored Division (U.S.), 56, 98,
    107
4th Infantry Division (U.S.), 22, 75,
    89
14th Cavalry Group, 89
43rd Infantry (British), 79
49th Infantry Division (British), 73
422nd Regiment (U.S.), 90, *91*
423rd Regiment (U.S.), 90, *91*
France
  citizens of, killed in allied invasion,
    18–19
  German invasion of, 10
  and partitioning of Germany, 115
  southern
    German evacuation of, 69
    invasion of, 18
Frank, Anne, 117
U.S.S. *Frankford,* 27
Free French, and liberation of Paris, 59
French army, on Sword Beach, 32–33
French Canadian soldiers, *9*
French navy, destruction of, 15

French Republic
  and partitioning of Germany, 115
  provisional government of, 59
French Riviera, assault on, 68–69, *68*
Friendly fire, casualties due to,
    55–56, 117
Frost, John, 76
Führerbunker, 103, 119

G
G-2, 72, 87, 91, 108. *See also* Allied
    intelligence
Gammon grenades, *42*
Garand rifles. *See* M-1 Garand rifles
Gas shortage, Allied, in race for West
    Wall, 65–67
Gault, James, 21
Gavin, James, 77–78, 119
General Motors, 27
George VI of England, 70
German air force. *See* Luftwaffe
German army. *See also*
    Counteroffensives, German
  Blitzkrieg tactics of, 10
  cruelty of, 10, 97
    at concentration camps, *115,*
    117–118, 119
  disarray of, in final weeks, *113*
  evacuation of southern France, 69
  executions of German soldiers by,
    198
  ferocity of, 106, 123
  during invasion of Germany, 114
  infantry at Normandy, 20–21
  invasion of Denmark and Norway,
    10
  invasion of France and
    Netherlands, 10
  looting by, *87*
  manpower shortages in, 72–73
  mines laid by, 20, *25,* 88, 106
  morale of, 20
    after Ardennes, 108
  Panzer reserves
    deployment of, 50
    positioning of, 20–21
  port strategy of, *63,* 63–64, *65*
  preparations for invasion, *19,*
    19–21,
  and prisoners, killing of, 93, 97
  as prisoners, *32, 100*
    and fear of Russians, 122, *122*
  Russia, invasion of, 11
  sabotage by, *109*
  strategy against invasion, 20
  tank corps, father of, *103*
  winter offensives, cost of, 99
German atrocities, at concentration
    camps, *115,* 117–118,
    119
German casualties. *See* Casualties
German deceptions, 29, 83, 93,
    95–96
German defenses, *25, 29, 51, 74*
  behind Atlantic Wall, 39–40

German equipment
  antiaircraft guns
    20mm, self-propelled, *98*
    88mm, *25,* 47, 76, *47, 92*
  antitank weapons, 72–73
  artillery, *23*
  horse-drawn, *83*
  1944 machine pistols, 72
  mg42 (Spandau) machine gun, *94*
  tanks, 45
    Mark IV, *29, 42*
    Mark V (Panther), 45, *83*
    Tiger (Mark VI), 45, 47, 117
    Tiger II (Royal Tiger), *83, 92, 93*
  Whirlwind anti aircraft gun, *98*
German intelligence, disinformation
    campaign against, 18
German mines, 20, *25,* 88, 106
German submarine service, father of,
    122
Germany
  Allied invasion of, 100–123
    stop line for, 117
    troop strength for, 104
  cipher codes of,
    Allied interception of, 18, 50,
    56, 73, 91
  decimation of, *121*
  declaration of war with U.S., 11
  defeat of, 101–123
  invasion of Russia, 11
  non-aggression pact with Russia,
    10
  partitioning of, 104
    and France, 115
  surrender of, *122,* 122–123
Germany first policy, 8, 11
Gerow, Leonard, 88, 117
Gliders
  Allied, 75, 77
  American, *20, 41*
  British, 21, *40*
  in Operation Varsity, 114
Glover, L. C., 32
Goebbels, Joseph, *10,* 119
Gold Beach, 30, *34*
Göring, Hermann, *10*
  desire to surrender, 119
Götterdämerung, influence of, on
    Hitler, 119
Grease guns (M3), *80*
Great Britain. *See* Britain
Grenadier Guards, 77
Grimball, John, 108
Ground force, largest ever
    commanded by
    American, 117
Grow, Robert W., 63
Guards Armored Division, *76*
Guderian, Heinz, 50, 101, *103*

H
Harbors, artificial, 45–46, *47*
Harmon, Ernest, 96
Hasbrouck, Robert W., 96
Hausser, Paul, 109
Hauteclocque, Jacques-Philippe, 59

Haute-Fagnes-Eifel area, German
    parachute drop over, 96
Hedgerows, battle of, 39–40, *40, 41*
  casualties in, 40
Hell's Highway, *76,* 76–77
Himmler, Heinrich, *10,* 119
History of Frederick the Great
    (Carlyle), 119
Hitler, Adolf, *10*
  assassination attempt against, 52
    recovery from, 70
  cruelty of, 10
  final days of, 119
  on German counteroffensive of
    December, 1944, 81
  gods of, 13
  influence of *Götterdämerung* on,
    119
  mistress of, 119
  Nero decree of, 109–111
  nihilism of, 111
  officer's opinion of, 20
  order to burn Paris, 59
  "port strategy" of, *63,* 63–64, *65*
  reaction to Allied invasion, 39, 53
  suicide of, 119
  on surrender, 81
  underground bunker of, 103, 119
    120
Hobart, Percy, 32
Hobart's funnies, 32, *33*
Hodges, Courtney H., 58, *69,* 72, 88,
    90, 96
Hoge, William, 108
Holland, operations in, *9*
Honan, Josh, 31
Hopkins, Harry, 15
Horrocks, Brian, 61, 78, 96, 105
Horse-drawn artillery, German, *83*
Houffalize, 101
Howard, John, 21, 34
101st Airborne (U.S.), 91
  at Bastogne, 97–98
  Hell's highway and, *76,* 76–77
  and invasion of Normandy, 20, 21,
    20–22, *43, 50*
Hürtgen Forest offensive, *59,* 85–88

I
Infantry divisions, U.S. *See also spe-*
    cific divisions
  composition of, 85
  house-to-house fighting of, *66*
  odds faced by, 85
Invasion of Germany, 100–123
  stop line for, 117
  troop strength for, 104
Invasion at Normandy. *See* Allied
    invasion of Brittany (D-day)
Irish Guards, 76
Italy
  Allied campaigns in, 11, 15
  declaration of war with U.S., 11

J
Japan
  bombing of Pearl Harbor, 8, 11
  bombing of Singapore, 8, 11

war against, 104
JCS (Joint Chiefs of Staff), 11
Jedlicka, Joseph, 78
Jodl, Hans, 122
Joint Chiefs of Staff (JCS), 11
Jones, Allan, 90
Jullouville, Eisenhower's head-
quarters at, 70
Juno Beach, 31

K
Kampfgruppe Peiper, 92–93
Kangaroos, 105–106
Keitel, Wilhelm, 55, 122
and German surrender, 122
war-crimes trial of, 122
Kesselring, Albert, 109, 110
HMS Kimberly, 68
King, Ernest J., 15
Köchling, Friedrich, 115
Koenig, Marie Pierre, 18, 59
Kotzebue, Albert L., 118
Krupp, Inc., 47
Krupp 88mm antiaircraft gun, 47, 47
Kuhn, Jack, 29

L
Landing craft, shortage of, 18
Landing craft tanks (LCTs)
American, 22
British, 9
Landing ship tanks (LSTs)
American, 18
shortage of, 18
Landing sites, D-Day
linking of, 37
selection of, 17, 17
Landing vehicle tracks (LVTs), 105
Largest ground force ever command
ed by American, 117
Latrell, Joseph, 99
Leclerc, Philippe, 59, 59
LeHavre, liberation of, 73
Leigh-Mallory, Trafford, 16
Leonard, John, 107–108
Liese, Joe, 107
Lomell, Leonard, 29
Long Toms, 63
Looting by German soldiers, 87
Lord Moran, 103
Lorient, siege of, 73
Lovat, Lord, 33
Low countries
German invasion of, 10
liberation of, 64
LSTs. See Landing ship tanks
Ludendorff railway bridge, 107
Luftwaffe, 78, 117
efforts to control, 8
and English air space, 10–11
founders of, 110
LVTs. See Landing vehicle tracks

M
M-1 Garand rifles, 21
M3 grease guns, 80
M-4 Sherman tanks, 45, 45, 79
M-10 Tank Destroyer, 90

Maginot Line, 20, 34
Malta Conference, 103–104
Mann, Joe E., 76–77
Mark V (Panther) tanks (German),
45, 83
Mark IV Churchill tank (British),
106
Mark IV tanks (German), 29, 42
Mark VI (Tiger) tanks (German), 45,
47, 117
Marseilles, liberation of, 68
Marshall, George C., 14, 15, 69, 85
Mauthausen concentration camp,
liberation of, 115
McAuliffe, Anthony, 97–98
McCrory, James "Paddy," 77
McNair, Leslie J., 56, 90
Mediterranean campaigns, 9, 11, 15
Merderet River, 22
MG42 (Spandau) machine gun, 94
Middleton, Troy, 56, 89, 90
Military Police, 109
Military tribunal at Nuremberg, 122
Milliken, John, 107
Millin, Bill, 33
Million dollar wounds, 85
Mills-Roberts, Derek, 114
Mims, Robert L., 109
Mine detectors, 106
Mines, German, 20, 25
Bouncing Betty type, 88
Shoe-mines, 106
Mobile warfare. See also Blitzkrieg
Allied, Hitler's fear of, 53, 56
Model, Wilhelm, 70, 73, 75, 115
Montgomery, Bernard Law, 16, 72
and assault on Caen, 48–52
background of, 16
as commander, at Battle of the
Bulge, 96–97
delivery of supplies to, 67
and German surrender, 122
and invasion of Germany, 117
on Normandy invasion, 37
and port at Antwerp, 73
promotion of, 70
and promotion of Bradley, 72
and race for West Wall, 65
reaction to Broad Front strategy,
69–70
Morale of German army, 20
after Ardennes, 108
Morgan, Frederick, 16
Mott, Hugh, 108
Mulberries, 17, 45–46
Mussolini, Benito, 73
fall of, 15

N
Nazi leaders, 10. See also specific
leaders
Nero decree, 109–111
Netherlands
German invasion of, 10
liberation of, 64
Neufmoulin, 95
The New York Times, 69
Nihilism of Hitler, 111

Nijmegen, bridge at, 77, 77–78, 78
9th Armored Division, 89, 108
9th Army Engineers (U.S.), 111
9th Infantry Division, 60
Ninth Army (U.S.), 73, 90, 96, 104,
108, 114, 115–117, 117
9th SS Panzer Division (German), 52,
75
IX Tactical Air Command, 93
9th Tactical Air Force (U.S.), 56
IX Troop Carrier Command, 67
90th Infantry Division (U.S.), 40
90-division gamble, Allied, 85, 98, 99
90mm guns (British), 77
90mm guns (U.S.), 46
99th Infantry Division (U.S.), 86, 88,
90
Niven, David, 34
Noel, Jacqueline, 33
Non-aggression pact between
Germany and Russia, 10
Nordhausen Concentration Camp,
liberation of, 117
Normandy beach
defenses of, 19
invasion of, 13–33
North Africa
Allied campaigns in, 11
American involvement in, 9
invasion of, 15
Norway, German invasion of, 10
Nuremberg
capture of, 121
military tribunal at, 122
Nurse Corps, U.S., 42

O
Ohrdruf Nord Concentration Camp,
117–118
Omaha Beach, 12, 23–29, 25, 28, 39
casualties on, 23
equipment losses on, 24
mulberry at, 46, 47
101st Airborne (U.S.), 20, 21, 20–22,
32, 50, 76–77, 76, 91,
at Bastogne, 97–98
Hell's highway and, 76, 76–77
and invasion of Normandy, 20, 21,
20–22, 43, 50
102nd Cavalry Reconnaissance
Squadron, 45
105mm howitzer (U.S.), 49
106th Infantry Division (U.S.), 89,
90, 91, 96
155mm guns (U.S.), 63
175th Rifle Regiment, 118
Oosterbeek, 78–79
Opening of World War II, 10
Operation Anvil, 18, 68
Operation Autumn Fog, 83
Operation Dragoon, 18, 68, 68–69
Operation Epsom, 52, 54
Operation Goodwood, 54, 55–56
Operation Grenade, 104, 105–106
Operation Herbstnebel, 83
Operation Market-Garden, 64, 74–79
Operation Nordwind, 98–99

Operation Overlord, 13, 55
origins of, 16–17
plan for, 65
transportation planning for, 67
Operation Plunder, 111–114
Operation Torch, 15
Operation Varsity, 114
casualties in, 114
Operation Veritable, 105–106
Operation Watch on the Rhine, 83
Osttruppen (Eastern troops), 21, 31

P
P-47 thunderbolt aircraft, 93–95, 98
P-51 aircraft, 117
Pacific war, 8
Paluch, Ted, 97
Panther tanks, 45, 83
Panzer Brigade 95, 150
Panzer Group West (German), 53
destruction of headquarters of, 50
Panzer Lehr Division (German), 50
destruction of, 56
Panzer reserves
deployment of, 50
positioning of, 20–21
Pappas, Ernest, 120
Parachute drop, German, over Haute-
Fagnes-Eifel area, 96
Paris
liberation of, 59, 59
supply of, after liberation, 67
Pas de Calais
defenses of, 19
as potential invasion site, 17, 18
Patch, Alexander, 68, 96
Patton, George S., Jr., 31, 56, 96, 120
advance of, 56, 58, 109
on Allied advance, 107
and concentration camps, 117–118
crossing of Rhine by, 109
delivery of supplies to, 67
fuel shortages and, 75
and German counteroffensive, 91
relief from command, 120
as strategist, 56
Pearl Harbor, bombing of, 8, 11
Peiper, Jochen, 92, 93
"Phony war," 10
Piauge, Robert, 33
Ploesti oil complex, 72
Point-du-Hoc, 26, 29
Poland
and German cipher codes, 18
German invasion of, 10
partitioning of, 10
Pontoon bridges, 108, 109, 111
Ports, effect of Red Ball Express on,
67–68
Port strategy of Hitler, after liberation
of Paris, 63, 63–64, 65
Prisoners
German, 32, 100
German execution of, 93, 97
Provisional Government of the
French Republic, 59
Pyle, Ernie, 56

Q
Quesada, Elwood "Pete," 93

R
The Racial Observer (Völkischer
Beobachter), 111
Railroads, French, German destruc
tion of, 63, 64
Ramcke, Hermann B., 63
Ramsay, Bertram, 16, 73
Rangers (U.S.), 26, 29. See also
Airborne units
2nd Ranger Battalion, 28
Rauschning, Hermann, 119
Razich-Blackburn-Tompkins Bridge,
109
Red army. See Russian army
Red Ball Express, 65, 65–66
Regiment de Maisonneuve, 9
Regina Rifle Regiment, 31
Reichswald, 106
clearing of, 105
Remagen Bridge, 107, 108, 108, 109
Rennie, Thomas, 114
Replacement troops, shortage of, 50
Reserves, German lack of, 99
Rheinmettal, Inc., 47
Rhine river
closing of, 104–105
crossing of, 103, 106–108, 112,
113
Rhinos, 45, 45, 60
Rijssen, 9
Roads, impassable, 104
Robertson, William D., 119
Robinson, Peter, 78
Rose, Maurice, 117
Royal Engineers, 111
Royal Tiger (Tiger II) tanks, 83, 92,
93
Ruhr
Allied assault on, 69
Hitler's intent to destroy, 111
reduction of, 114–115
Ruhr pocket, resistance in, 115
Rumania
anti-Nazi coup in, 70
surrender of, 72–73
Rupinski, Frank, 29
Russia
anti-Red (Osttruppen) elements in,
21, 31

casualties in capture of Berlin, 117
contribution on eastern front, 9
German invasion of, 11
non-aggression pact with Germany, 10
and surrender of Germany, 122
Russian army
assault on Berlin, 119
ineffectiveness of, 11
losses of, 11
meeting up with American forces, *118,* 118–119
size of, 11
winter offensive (1945), 99, 101

S

Saar Offensive, *90*
Sabotage, German, *109*
Sachsenhausen, *113*
St. Lô, assault on, 55, *55*
Scheldt Estuary, German resistance in, 73, 74
Schlemm, Alfred, 106
Scorched earth policy, German, 109
Seaborne, Ronald, 30
2nd Armored Division (France), *31, 59*
2nd Armored Division (U.S.), 96, 117, *120*
Second Army (British), 60, 105, *105,* 114
2nd Corps (Canadian), 105
Second front
Allied caution in opening, 15
Russian calls for, 11
2nd Infantry Division (U.S.), *86,* 88
2nd Parachute Division (German), 63
2nd Ranger Battalion (U.S.), *28*
2nd SS Panzer Division (German), 56
716th Division (German), 31
719th Division (German), 7
17th Airborne Division (U.S.), 114
7th Armored Division (British), 51, *123*
7th Armored Division (U.S.), *95,* 96
Seventh Army (German), 65
destruction of, 58–59
Seventh Army Group (Allied), 91
Seventh Army (U.S.), 68, 69, 98
7th Corps (U.S.), *23,* 56
75th Infantry Division (U.S.), *80*
SHAEF. *See* Supreme Headquarters Allied Expeditionary Force
Sherman tanks, *60, 83, 100*
M-4, 45, *45, 79*
Shoe-mines, German, 106
U.S.S. *Shubrick,* 27
Shuh-mines, German, 106
Sicily, Allied campaigns in, 11, 15
Siegfried Line, 105. *See* West Wall
origin of name, 79
Silesia, capture of, 106
Simonds, Guy, 105
Simpson, William H., *72,* 96, 106
Singapore, Japanese bombing of, 11
6th Airborne (British), 21, 32, 114
6th Armored Division (U.S.), 56, 63, *113*

Sixth Army Group (U.S.), 69, 91, 98
Sixth Panzer Army (German), 85, *86,* 91, 92
Sixth Panzer Division (German), 88
6th SS Panzer Army, 92
69th Division, First Army (U.S.), first meeting with Russians, 118–119
63rd Infantry Division (U.S.), *116*
Skorzeny, Otto, 95
Slave laborers, German, 117
Smith, Walter Bedell, 16, 97
Snipers, German, 30, *51, 105*
Soviet Union. *See* Russia
Spandau (MG42) machine gun, *94*
Spaulding, John, 27
Speer, Albert, 103, 111
Spitfire aircraft, 59
Spring thaw, and impassable roads, *104*
SS
in Ardennes, 92–96
brutality of, 92, 93
storm troopers of, *99*
St. Nazaire, siege of, 73
St. Vith, *88,* 96
Allied recapture of, *95*
Stalin, Josef, 11, *103*
and Teheran Conference, 15, *16*
and Yalta Conference, *103,* 103–104
Steele, John, 22
Stimson, Henry L., 69, 85
Stomach battalions, 21
Strasbourg, 98
Student, Kurt, 73, *73*
Submarine warfare in Atlantic, 8, 11
Suez Canal, opening of, 11
Supply problems, Allied, 65, 73
Support units, *24*
Supreme commander of Allied Expeditionary Force, 13–16
Supreme Headquarters Allied Expeditionary Force (SHAEF), 16, 72, 73, 87, 90, 97
insignia for, 8
Surrender of German army
and fear of Russians, 122, *122*
Hitler on, 81
Sword Beach, 31–34, *40*

T

T-26 Pershing tanks, 108
Tanks, 45, *45,* 92
Comet, *114*
Firefly, 45
Landing craft tank (LCT)
American, *22*
British, *9*
Landing ship tanks (LSTs)
American, *18*
M-10 Tank Destroyer (U.S.), *90*
Mark V (Panther) tanks (German), 45, 83
Mark IV Churchill tank (British), *106*
Mark IV tanks (German), *29, 42*
Mark VI (Tiger) tanks (German), 45, 47, 117

Sherman, *60, 83, 100*
M-4, 45, *45, 79*
T-26 Pershing tanks, 108
Tiger II (Royal Tiger) (German), 83, 92, *93*
Taylor, George, 27
Taylor, Maxwell, 77, 97
Tedder, Arthur, 16
Teheran Conference, 15, *16*
Teller mines, 20, *25*
10th Armored Division (U.S.), 98
10th SS Panzer Division (German), 52, 75, 77
3rd Algerian Division (French), 98, 115
3rd Armored Division (U.S.), *79, 80,* 117
Third Army (U.S.), *31,* 58, 69, 90, 96, *99,* 107, *107,* 110, *112, 113,* 117
III Corps, 107
3rd Infantry Division (British), 31–32, *34*
3rd Infantry Division (Canada), 31, 73, 105
13th Field Hospital, *42*
30th Division (U.S.), 56
30 Corps (British), 61, 96, 105
325th Parachute Infantry Regiment (U.S.), *41*
Tiger II (Royal Tiger) tanks, 83, 92, *93*
Tiger (Mark VI) tanks, 45, 47, 117
Timmerman, Karl, 108
Tobruk, fall of, 15
Todt, Fritz, 79
Topley, Earl, *51*
Toulon
bombardment of, *68*
liberation of, 68, *74*
Transport aircraft, 75
Transportation Corps (U.S.), 67
Transportation Plan, 64
Treadway bridges, 108, 111
Trenches, warfare in, *73*
Trench foot, 88
Trois-Ponts, 93
12th Army Group (Allied), *56,* 58, 63–64, 69, 72, 91, 117
Twenty Committee (XX), 18
21st Army Group (Allied), 48, 69, 73, 105, 111, 114
casualties during Operation Varsity, 114
21st Panzer Division (German), 34, 51
28th Infantry Division (U.S.), *36,* 59, 88, 89, 96
29th Infantry Division (U.S.), 23, 27
285th Field Artillery Observation Battalion (U.S.), 93, 97
290th Infantry Regiment (U.S.), *80*
Typhoon aircraft, 34, 50, 59

U

U-boats, German, 8, 11
Ultra, Allied interception of, 18, 50, 56, 73, 91

Underground bunker of Hitler, 103, 119
United States
domination of, in final weeks of war, 117
Germany's declaration of war against, 11
United States equipment
of Airborne units, 21, *21*
Buffaloes, 105
C-47 aircraft, 98
Dukws, 26, *27,* 105, *112*
gliders, *20, 41*
Kangaroos, 105
Landing craft tanks (LCTs), *22*
Landing ship tanks (LSTs), *18*
Landing vehicle tracks (LVTs), 105
M-1 Garand rifles, 21
M3 grease guns, *80*
M-10 Tank Destroyer, *90*
90mm guns (U.S.), *46*
105mm howitzer (U.S.), *49*
P-47 Thunderbolt aircraft, 93–95, 98
P-51 aircraft, 117
rhinos, 45, *45, 60*
T-26 Pershing tanks, 108
tanks, 45, *45, 99*
Sherman, *60, 83, 100*
M-4, 45, *45, 79*
trucks
shortage of, during race for West Wall, 67
United States forces. *See also specific units*
African-American soldiers in, 24
airborne units, 21–22
equipment of, 21, *21*
casualties. *See* Casualties
exhaustion of, prior to Battle of the Bulge, 85
inexperience of, 8–9
infantry divisions
composition of, 85
house-to house fighting of, *66*
odds faced by, 85
meeting up with Russians, *118,* 118–119
United States generalship, low point of, 85
United States Navy, 111
Upper Silesia, 101
Urquhart, Robert E., 75
U.S. *See* United States
Utah Beach, 22, *22,* 23, *23,* 31, *41*
casualties on, 23

V

V-E Day, 122
Victory, glimpses of, 61–62, 72
Victory in Europe Day, 122
Völkischer Beobachter (The Racial Observer), 111
von Choltitz, Dietrich, 59
von der Heydte, Friedrich, 96
von Kluge, Günther, *54,* 55, 56, 58, 70
von Manteuffel, Hasso, 85, *86,* 96, 99

von Rundstedt, Gerd, 20, 53, 54, 73, *93,* 106
in Battle of the Bulge, 91
firing of, 108–109
reaction to Operation *Herbstnebel* plan, 85
von Rundstedt Offensive, 82–83, 93
von Schleiben, Karl Wilhelm, 48
von Schweppenburg, Freiherr Geyr, 53, 54
von Stauffenberg, Klaus, 52

W

Wacht am rhein, 83–84
Waco gliders, 20
Walcheren Island, 73, 74
operations on, *9*
Waldenburg, *116*
Wall, Herman, *28*
War of attrition (Nov. 1944), 85
HMS *Warspite,* 32
"Water Rats," 105
Weather
and Battle of the Bulge, 83, *84*
cold, protection from, *94*
and mud, 105, *104*
and Operation Market-Garden, *76*
pre-Normandy invasion, 19
Wehrmacht. *See* German army
West Wall, *62,* 72
assault on, 79
construction of, 79
defense of, 73, *73*
German flight to, 61–79, *62, 65*
Whirlwind anti aircraft gun, 98
Wierzbowski, Edward L., 76–77
Wilhelmina Canal, *76,* 77
Wilson, Charles, *103*
Winter offensives in Ardennes, cost of, to Germans, 99
Wittman, Michael, 51
Wobelein Concentration Camp, *119*
Wojtusik, Stanley, 90
Wood, Eric Fisher, Jr., 89
World War II, opening of, 10
Wounded, caring for, *35. See also* Casualties
Wright brothers, *44*

Y

Yalta Conference, *103,* 103–104, 115, 117

Z

Zec, Philip, 72
Zhukov, Georgi, 101, 122
Zimmerit paste, *42*